UTZON

AND THE

SYDNEY

OPERA

HOUSE

PHILIP DREW

CONTENTS

INTRODUCTION

This book is based on six years research into Jørn Utzon and related events surrounding the design, documentation, politics and finances of the Sydney Opera House. In the beginning I was motivated to find answers to a number of accusations levelled against Utzon by politicians and others, some coming from the client Labor government, but mostly, emanating from the NSW Liberal/Country Party Coalition Opposition under Robert Askin, which subsequently replaced Labor in government after 1965 and forced him to withdraw permanently from the project nine months later in February 1966.

There was a general perception, fostered by the Askin government, that Utzon, for all his brilliance, was responsible for each and every problem, and that he consequently, must go. His departure, therefore, was seen by many at the time as confirming this analysis of a dilatory architect who was unable to come to grips with actually building his masterpiece. This, it was felt, should be carried out by essentially practical men, namely, Ove Arup & Partners under the astute and responsible direction of the new Public Works Minister, Davis Hughes. This prevailing view must now be challenged in the light of new research by myself and others, which overwhelmingly points to a substantial political failure rather than an architectural one. This is not to say there were not problems, there were plenty of these, but what made the difference was a divided Labor party, the death of Cahill in 1959 at the beginning of the project which left it rudderless, and an opposition which opportunistically treated the Opera House issue as an electoral springboard to win office.

The story is not merely about architecture, to treat it as such is to miss what really happened, it was as much about politics as it was about architecture. The text is presented in the form of a series of notes, each condensed so it registers like a frame in a movie, which when assembled, fuses into a flowing depiction of events. Each note is flagged by a date so the reader can build an interpretation of when, who, where, what happened into an impression much like the rungs of a ladder takes us from a beginning to our destination, gradually completing through the accretion of historical details a comprehensive understanding of the unfolding pattern of events. These are given in the chronological order in which they happened, each individual is named, and locations identified. This information has been supplied with little or no interpretation or prodding from myself with the intention of allowing readers to arrive at their own judgements and conclusions independently.

Obviously, the inclusion of some events or the omission of others affects this process; it would be ideal to include everything, however, this is impractical, therefore in the interest of economy, I have left some things out and limited the amount of the information so as not to confuse readers and to give the text a focus. But, as much as possible, I wanted to give all the important facts to readers and allow the evidence to tell its story. As much as possible, I avoided colouring events with my own reading of history. It is possible I have included too much information, but I thought that was preferable to not providing enough.

Till now, for all the passion engendered by Utzon's departure, the interpretation of what occurred in 1965 to 1966, has been bedevilled by insufficient research and the determination by many people, to distort the facts in order to make them fit an already fixed position. As a consequence, the truth was submerged under a flood tide of bias. This book has been published in the hope of pushing back that tide and revealing the decisive evidence to give an entirely new reading of history, founded on the salient facts.

The doubts expressed about Utzon's architectural performance amounted to accusations about his dedication, temperament, motivation — the longer it took and the more the project cost, the more fees he would be paid — and ultimately, his architectural competence. Few of the politicians who were involved, understood the unprecedented technical challenge of Utzon's design, or the limitations of structural and acoustical analysis and modelling procedures. There has been no examination of the quantity surveyor, Rider Hunt and Partners' performance, why so many of its estimates proved unreliable. No one blamed the quantity surveyor for giving unreliable estimates. When blame was allocated, it was heaped on Utzon because he was most visible, and because the public did not understand how an architect works, or the important role of consultants. There has been no attempt, after all this time, to check the roof vaults to see whether they could not have been made far more efficient and cheaply. Utzon became the scapegoat for any and all the problems that arose. In many instances, problems were caused not by Utzon, but by local political factors, cowardice and ignorance.

It was said at the time that Utzon was a brilliant designer, but that he was impractical, that he did not know how to construct what he designed. Today, when the construction industry is so much more capable, and almost anything can be built, this seems especially hollow. At the time, many people were greatly influenced by such accusations. The charge of practical and financial incompetence repeatedly levelled against Utzon by the Minister for Public Works, Davis Hughes, backed by the Government Architect, Edward Farmer, and by many senior members of the Sydney architectural fraternity were never actually proved.

In retrospect, the Sydney Opera House was a bargain. Its initial cost dwindles compared to the moneys spent on a major upgrade, the forecourt construction work, and the underground car park. Utzon spent a mere $18.4 million on the first two stages, out of the total expenditure of $102 million. By contrast, Davis Hughes spent $83.6 million on just the third stage — 4½ times Utzon and was forced in the latter stages to borrow money. This should make people stop and think before accusing Utzon of behaving irresponsibly. These days the public is justifiably more distrustful of what politicians claim. They should be. Davis Hughes squandered millions to save face. In the game of politics, Utzon's reputation was of little concern.

The picture of Utzon as an impractical idealist, who could not make decisions on time, has unfortunately stuck. Politicians and government alike had a vested interest in blaming Utzon and it was largely successful. The project was carried out against a critically unstable political backdrop which constantly questioned the worth of such an ambitious cultural undertaking. It was attacked chiefly in terms of its high cost, and this imposed a severe burden on Utzon, because Utzon became the inevitable focus of community doubts about the wisdom of the moneys being spent.

In March 1967, Donald Horne, writing in a publication edited by University of New South Wales academic, Elias Duek–Cohen, defended Utzon against the main accusations which he summarised as:

Utzon is a brilliant architect,

BUT

Utzon was insisting on the wrong organisational approach.

Utzon ignores questions of time.

Utzon ignores questions of cost.

Utzon is not a practical man.

In the aftermath of Utzon's resignation on 28 February 1966, his Sydney supporters attempted to neutralise the Askin government's criticisms with its own facts — but unfortunately it had little practical effect as it was a case of too little too late. The crucial and decisive decision about turning the Main Hall had into a single purpose auditorium had already been made by Davis Hughes some time before the Duek–Cohen booklet was released.

The Utzon defence characterised the Minister as incompetent, dissimulating, and obstructionist; it asserted, moreover, that his interference made matters worse, not better; that he had deliberately undermined Utzon's position professionally, withheld fees owed him, and caused Utzon unwarranted financial hardship; that he refused to give permission for the plywood mock–ups for the ceilings of the halls and the glass wall mullions to proceed, which directly threatened the future of the job; that he was jealous of Utzon and wanted to replace him in order to capture the public limelight; and that he ultimately conspired against Utzon to remove him from the project and that this did irreparable damage to Utzon's professional reputation internationally.

In pursuing my research, I came across evidence for a number of new insights which radically changed the historical picture:

The greatest financial scandal occurred not while Utzon was in charge, but afterwards in 1972–73, under the management of the Askin government while Davis Hughes was responsible when the government was forced to borrow A\$22 million from treasury to complete the project. Afterwards, the Opera House was handicapped by the lack of work–as–executed drawings and the approach to the Opera House suffered from sub–standard asphalt paving and an improvised temporary covered way access.

Documents confirmed there had been a ministerial conspiracy approved by the Cabinet and the Premier to remove Utzon in August 1965. These set out in detail, step by step, the actions which were to be implemented and the Askin government adhered to this scenario to a remarkable degree. Davis Hughes at first implemented this plan hesitantly, then with increasing ruthlessness to bring it to its fateful conclusion in February 1966. Once the plan was accepted by cabinet, there was never even the remote possibility of the government turning back or asking Utzon to return.

It was known at the time that Davis Hughes' rejection of opera in the Major Concert Hall was unnecessary and emasculated the usefulness of the Opera Centre as a performing arts venue, while the time lost in making the changes added enormously to the project's ultimate cost and delayed still further its completion. Davis Hughes' changes cannot be reversed, indeed, the crippling effect on the Opera House's functionality are irreversible, all that can be done now by way of improving the situation amounts to little more than palliative surgery. The real cost of his intervention was much more than the muddying of the aesthetic purity of Utzon's vision, it represented a severe amputation and curtailment of its function.

The actual reason for Utzon's departure was never revealed and was due to entirely different circumstances only partly connected with his conflict with the Minister for Public works.

Very little was known about Davis Hughes' political career before this, especially about his character, political connections, flaws and influences. This gap has been remedied. For example, Bill Wheatland's (Utzon's office manager) father, was Davis Hughes' superior officer in the RAAF during World War Two, but Wheatland unaccountably made no use of this source.

Until now, we have been entirely dependent on Utzon for our understanding of the design references in the prize Sydney Opera House scheme in 1956. Concurrent with tracing Utzon's family background and history, his training and travels, other equally crucial sources presented themselves. With this in mind, it is possible to understand now why the Opera House is such a richly expressive work. However, the most significant contribution of the new research is what it reveals about who Utzon was, his strategy of resigning in order to be called back on his own terms which misfired, his double tax problems which made all the plan irrelevant, and how he approached design.

It was clear that the text needed to be arranged in an easily read format. Information about Utzon, the Sydney Opera House, events, people, politics, design and engineering advances, costs and construction has been presented in the right column text chronologically, including later developments after Utzon left in 1966. Dates for these entries are placed alongside on the left. To further assist readers, a series of ikons have been introduced left of the date column to indicate specific Utzon achievements. Within the main text I have included capsules on significant individuals, related topics and firsts. People's names (where accompanied by a capsule), era defining events which reveal the mood of each period, Utzon projecs etc., have been flagged by bold type. The amounts paid to Utzon as fees have been underlined throughout.

Because of the accusation about time and costs, estimates of cost, completion dates, fees paid to Utzon and other related financial matters, where available, fees paid to Utzon are included with notes on any delays and difficulties arising from the non–payment of fees.

It is hoped that in publishing a full account of architecture, politics, people, events, and finances from a wide range of documentary sources, readers can quickly find answers to a question, check a particular event. The Sydney Opera House story is such an intriguing mixture of human imagination, engineering and building innovation on so many levels, politics and the performing arts, the challenge was to bring all these separate aspects together simultaneously. This was the aim: whether it succeeds, whether the answers are there in the detail, is for the reader to decide.

PHILIP DREW
SEPTEMBER 2000

At his farewell party Utzon was given a boomerang to encourage him to return to Australia and finish the Opera House. Photo by Ellias Duek–Cohen.

Nyhavn. H.C. Andersen and Utzon had rooms here.

JØRN UTZON'S SCANDINAVIAN MAGIC

Jørn Utzon, the Dane who designed the opera house, is many things: an irrepressible storyteller and artist who, like his fellow countryman, Hans Christian Andersen, could be a great charmer. He is the quintessential Dane, as tall and handsome in his youth as any fairytale prince or Hollywood matinee idol.

It is an extraordinary story how, in 1956, a relatively unknown should have designed one of the great buildings of the 20th century for a site he had never seen, half the world away. How was it that so deliberately Scandinavian a building could be so right for Sydney? What is it about it that has transformed it into a universally recognised icon of the city?

Its creation contains many surprises and is as full of twists and turns as any fairy tale. It has a magic all its own, an enchantment that few do not feel. Its story reads like a fairy tale, a struggle between good and evil, in which the handsome prince was forced to abandon his greatest treasure to release himself from the evil wizard's spell. Ultimately, the Opera House's magic triumphed. As a fairy tale it is all the more powerful for being real.

Utzon reminds one of Hans Christian Andersen and Sören Kierkegaard by turns; he loved to spin tales and trick people for fun, yet, possessed the same honest directness of thought as the philosopher. Possibly it is the plainness of Danish daily life, possibly Anderson and Kierkegaard are typical of the Danish personality which Utzon shares. There is also a pervasive poetry to everything he does that lifts whatever he designs out of the ordinary.

To understand the Sydney Opera House one must start with where Utzon lived, where he studied, his family, training and background influences. This requires we undertake a journey of four centuries across Danish history from Utzon's earliest known ancestor, Ude Pedersen, who lived in Kolding, a castle–town on a fjord in the south–east coast of Jutland where his forebears comprised merchants, a quarter–master to a dragoon regiment and, several generations of dyers. Utzon grew up in Aalborg, a rough industrial city in north Jutland, and settled outside Hellebæk on the northern coast of Zealand. At the beginning of the 19th century Utzon's ancestors changed the spelling of their surname from 'Udsen' to 'Utzon'.

The Danish psyche is saturated by the sea from its constant exposure to sea life, ships and ship building, and sea traffic. Like many other Danes, Utzon is tied to the sea.

Denmark is a quirky country with a surprising underlying intensity to it. Utzon has a similar disarming casualness to him. He appears straightforward and lacking artifice, a man who is most contented when he is in nature.

The Sydney Opera House was an unlikely venture from the outset, yet it resulted in one of the most captivating buildings of the 20th century. Today, it is a monument and piece of sculpture so at home on its isolated peninsula one is reminded of Andersen's *Little Mermaid* on the Copenhagen Harbour waterfront who, according to the story, was a tiny creature who forsook the world of the "sea people" for a chance to win a human heart. In like manner, Utzon's much larger monument won the heart of Sydney, by engaging the maritime setting of the harbour and counterpoint to the statuesque and glittering office towers since arrayed to overlook it.

Few people have noticed how Danish, or, in general, how Scandinavian, the Opera House in Sydney is. What an extraordinary fluke Utzon's masterpiece was in 1956. Not only did it honour its location, it supplied a much needed symbol for the city that reflected its special maritime character. In this respect, it is like the gothic palazzi on Venice's canals, where architecture and water intermingle. You might say that it is the architectural equivalent of Sandro Botticelli's *Venus* emerging from the sea on her shell as she is blown towards Arcadia.

Utzon had never seen Sydney before the design, with no direct knowledge of the site he could only reconstruct it in his imagination from maritime charts and uninteresting halftone photographs. How did he manage to make the perfect match of architecture and harbour site half a world away? Was it a magnificent accident, or was it the fundamental Danish consciousness of the sea and ships that inflected Utzon's vision in a way none of the 230 other competitors could.

Denmark, Utzon's Scandinavian contacts and travels to the United States and the Yucatan, supply valuable insights into this fascinating puzzle and help to explain his sources for the Opera House.

In Denmark there exists an intimacy between water craft and architecture that is truly ancient. Nowhere is the sea far away. It permeates town life–boats and buildings are juxtaposed in town vistas, houses overlook harbours and canals and in 19th–century paintings, windows open on to picturesque views of ships masts and the clutter of rigging. Jørn Utzon's father was the chief engineer at the Aalborg shipyard before his promotion to director of the Helsingør shipyard in 1937. In his spare time, Aage Utzon designed a traditional type of Danish yacht called a *spidsgattere*, or double–ender — so named because its stern and bow were pointed. Growing up around shipyards, the distinction between naval architecture and regular architecture was blurred in Utzon's mind. His assumptions about architecture were indelibly shaped by the strenuous beauty, fitness, choice of materials, and fitness of ships to their purpose.

But it was the landscape of Denmark itself, which was the most critical factor when Utzon sat down in mid–1956 to design his scheme for the National Opera House international competition in Sydney. Utzon had previously completed a modest single–storey house in the Hammermill Wood beech forest adjoining Hellebæk village. With its high lakes, surrounding beech forest, brooks, and long languorous beaches, this is one of the most spectacularly beautiful parts of Denmark.

To the east, nearby, is Kronborg Castle, built by King Eric of Pomerania in 1425, and made famous by Shakespeare as Hamlet's haunted castle. It stands guard at the entrance of Øre Sund and the sea road to the Baltic Sea. Utzon had sailed around the castle innumerable times and admired the way its spires and towers shifted depending on his location. He admired the freedom of being on the water, the way the sky suddenly dominated everything, the formations of low hastening clouds that spilled upwards from a horizontal base line as they were gripped by faster moving air higher up. This was food for his imagination: the clouds as shell roofs, the terraces of Kronborg as the solid masonry platform for his opera and theatre halls.

Clouds over Kattegat at Hornbæk

Kronborg Castle from northwest

He poured these ideas into his sketches for the Sydney Opera House. Later, when he came to refine the scheme for the interior of the main hall, Utzon made a tiny sketch for his Japanese assistant, Yuzo Mikami, of the beech forest canopy which became the inspiration for the plywood ceiling of faceted triangular plates.

Some important architectural models were also local. In 1937, Utzon studied architecture at the Royal Academy of Art, which at that time was housed in Charlottenborg Palace on the south side of Kongens Nytor square in Copenhagen. Next to it was the Royal Opera House, which was a copy of the Vienna State Opera building. It faced the square, so it never occurred to Utzon to do otherwise in Sydney.

Consequently, his opera house is approached from the city and looks back at it, a feature that was exceptional compared to other competition entries.

On his return to Denmark, after three years in Stockholm to escape the German occupation, Utzon rented a flat on Rosenørns Allé close by the Broadcast House radio centre, which was completed in September 1945. It supplies several clues. Broadcast House and Utzon's later opera house have a number of features in common, thus, Utzon's shell concrete vaults were envisaged to be no thicker than 12.5 cm, with a second interior acoustic shell suspended from the outer shell. They both have a timber interior with red ox–hide upholstered seats. It was no coincidence that Wilhelm Jordan, the expert responsible for Broadcast House's acoustics, was subsequently hired by Utzon as his acoustic consultant for the Sydney halls.

In the 1930s, Denmark was a pioneer of shell concrete construction. The famous Mexican shell builder, Felix Candela, borrowed his shell calculations from Denmark. Shell concrete vaults spanning as much as 40 metres were a prominent design feature of Broadcast House and the 1939 traffic hall at Copenhagen's airport terminal. Utzon did not have to search far for his ideas; the most avant–garde works of modern architecture used shell concrete. Knowing this, his choice of shells for the Sydney Opera House comes as no surprise. The real departure, which moved many people, apart from the unexpectedness of the shell roofs at that time, was the sculptural expressiveness of their forms.

"Expressiveness" is critical not only in human relationships, but also in architecture where sculptural expressiveness ensures that the Opera House connects with people. To explain his conception of vaulting concrete shells surmounting 'the house', in 1957 Utzon said "I looked at flowers and insects, at organic forms. I wanted something that was growing out." What he meant was that architecture ought to be organic like nature and buildings should seem to have grown from the earth rather than to have been stuck there. One usage of "Express" is "To press out the contents of". The Opera House does appear to do this by pressing upwards off Bennelong Point and the theatres thrusting like seeds that press outwards and give rise to a unique arrangement of roof shapes that mirror the theatrical processes within them. Expressive architecture expresses its nature, it says what it is to us, what is going on within it. Expressiveness resembles well fitting clothing that partly conceals, and, also, partly reveals the contours of the body underneath.

At the beginning of the 1950s, a few years before Utzon made his design for the Sydney Opera House, Martin Heidegger, a German philosopher, thought that for humans to dwell in a place they needed to gather its spiritual qualities inside them.

Hammermill Wood beech forest, Hellebæk

Broadcast House, Rosenørns Allé

Sydney Opera House photographed from Govenor Phillip Tower

The identity, or 'spirit', ascribed to place means something more than location. Heidegger introduced the concepts of 'earth' and 'sky' to describe the identity or 'spirit' of place, and further stated that dwelling occurs between 'earth' and 'sky', in a zone he called the 'world'. Dwelling is being at peace with place in which the world becomes an 'inside'. The unusual composition of the Sydney Opera House as a platform surmounted by shell roofs that are metaphors for the earth and sky, with human performances presented on the platform in a zone between the platform/earth and roof/sky, exactly matches Heidegger's conditions for dwelling — for gathering the concrete qualities of world inside the human. It may be just an extraordinary coincidence, but that seems highly unlikely, or, it is more likely that Utzon intuitively grasped not only Heidegger's distinction of 'earth' and 'sky', but has used it to set the Sydney Opera House up in its place so people can feel serenely at peace with the Sydney landscape that is its setting.

Utzon has given numerous explanations for the shells, to which the public generously added its own colourful interpretations, but in a characteristically off–hand way, Utzon said that he was inspired by "life in the mountains and the life of the skier, the hunter in the woods, the Arab in the desert, the Indian, the Mexican…" He digresses with hunters and Arabs, but in referring to skiing and mountains, a reference to his winter holidays in central Sweden in 1943 and 1944, the shell roofs, far from being "sails," are likely snow covered mountains and hills or moguls.

Vilhelm Lauritzen's Broadcast House shells were regular shallow vaults or uniform corrugated waves, but Utzon freely composed his shells so they appear as sails or sea shells mounted on a rising platform that grows out of the rock of Bennelong Point. His shells are intensely rhythmical, the same basic shape is repeated and overlapped like a sequence of notes rising to a climax, which then subsides gently to a denouement in the free–standing restaurant out the front. Repeating the composition, and, placing each side by side, instead of end to end, the melody is played out before our eyes at a lower scale so we can appreciate its beauty for a second time.

The simplicity of the outside and accompanying restrained austerity inside is thoroughly Scandinavian. Utzon admired the Swedish modernist Gunnar Asplund and worked for a very brief time in 1945 with the Finnish master, Alvar Aalto, who had often visited Copenhagen for lectures, and who said, incidentally, that if he were to live in Denmark, he would choose to live in a beech forest. Utzon must have heard him!

Utzon's other great influences came from America. He was enchanted by Frank Lloyd Wright's demonstration of organic principle. The shells of the Opera House in Sydney attest to this in being far more horizontal than was structurally sensible. Utzon exaggerated the horizontal at the expense of structural logic. His other great encounter was with the ancient Mayan temple complexes on the Yucatan peninsula, which he visited in 1949. In particular, Monte Alban, a mountaintop complex of monuments on terraces linked by stairs, which supplied the idea for the grand staircase in front of the Sydney Opera House. It also supplied the important symbolic conception of a building as consisting of a base growing out of the earth, and lightweight roofs treated as voluptuously free forms representing a sky connection.

Monte Alban, reduced architecture to these two elements, a heavy earthbound stone platform, shrouded in swirling mist, and held in place by a magnificent sky.

Utzon's meeting with Eero Saarinen during his US trip was crucial for him. Saarinen's father, Eliel Saarinen, was a famous Finnish architect who emigrated to the US. Eero Saarinen later designed the TWA Terminal at J.F. Kennedy Airport as a freely sculptured concrete eagle, and his hanging roof at Dulles Terminal for Washington, D.C. was subsequently picked up by Utzon as a model for his Kuwait National Assembly. Eight years later, in January 1957, when Utzon was announced as the winner of the Sydney competition, only Saarinen among the jury knew Utzon well enough to describe him: "Utzon is a man about 42 to 44 years old [he was 38]. I met him several years ago — well, he is a tall very handsome Dane with blond hair, as most Danes have. I've seen several competition drawings which he has won and there is a very fine quality about his work. I've always considered him as one of the really most talented men in Scandinavia."

For both Andersen and Utzon, their fame was almost accidental, although justified in terms of their genius. Both were casualties of their own characters, as much as of circumstance. Utzon withdrew midway and failed to complete his greatest work. Andersen wanted to be a great writer of fiction but produced only great fairy tales, which he regarded as minor creations. If Anderson was the ugly duckling who transformed himself into a swan through his art, Utzon was a graceful swan gliding over life's pond, who was insufficiently pugnacious when challenged by politics. In spite of this defect, his place in 20th-century architecture and that of his beloved Sydney Opera House is assured.

The interiors of the Sydney Opera House were wrecked by the ignorance of politicians. In the 1960s Australia lacked the necessary cultural maturity to appreciate Utzon's vision. What was lost in 1967 can surely never be retrieved.

The result is a tragic masterpiece, a Scandinavian building in every sense, which gave meaning and a focus to a city that, before this, lacked one. Utzon's masterpiece awakened the city to itself, much the same as the prince's kiss brought Sleeping Beauty back to life.

UTZON'S ANCESTORS

1578 G.I Ude Pedersen (1578–1641) of Kolding, m. Maren Sørensdatter (1598 1640); eldest son Peder Udsen (4 children).

1616 G.II Peder Udsen (1616–1659), Kolding, m Dorothe Pedersdatter (4 children); second son Ude Pedersen.

N.D. G.III Ude Pedersen (–1707) student of theology, vicar for Gosmer & Halling (4 children: 2 sons, 2 daughters).

1679 G.IV Lauritz Udsen (1679–) 3 child of Ude Pedersen, m. Elisabeth Marie Hansdatter Leehman (1696), (5 children).

1727 G.V Peder Udsen (1727–) Kolding, m. Anne Birgitte Høstmarch (1740–1735) in 1762, buried in Flynder Church, 3 children. Peder Udsen became a regimental quartermaster.

1735 Church book records commence.

1781 G.VI Michael Lausen Utzon (1781–1854) Kolding, worked as a *farver*, m. Christine Jørgensen (1785–1849) in Kolding Church in 1804 (14 children).

1805 G.VII Nicholas Peder Utzon (1805–1880) *farver* of Kolding, m. Birgitte Marie Mathiesen (1813–1885) in 1837 (6 children).

1843 G.VIII Hans Jørgen Utzon, 3rd child (b. Ribe 1843–d. Hellebæk 1912), *farver* at Ribe, moves to Hellebæk early 1880s as *opsynmand* at Hellebæk factory, m. Anne Marie Christine Sønderborg (1846–1912), 3 children: Nicholai Peder Utzon (b. Ribe 1873–1941), Elisabeth Christine (B. Ribe 1877–), & Aage Oberg Utzon Hellebæk 1885–1970).

1885 G.IX Aage Oberg Utzon b. Hellebæk 1885–d. Hellebæk 1970), m. Estrid Valeska Halina Olsen (1894–1951), 3 children: Leif Oberg Utzon (b. Copenhagen 1916–d. Paris 1964), Jørn Oberg Utzon (b. Copenhagen 1918–), & Erik Oberg Utzon (b. Hellebæk 1924–d. Morocco 1955).

1918 G.X Jørn Oberg Utzon, born in Copenhagen (9 April 1918), m. Lis Fenger (b. 8 April 1919) in 1942 (Stockholm), 3 children: Jan Oberg Utzon (b. 27 September 1944–), Lin Oberg Utzon (b. 23 May 1946–), Kim Oberg Utzon (b. 1 Jan 1957–)

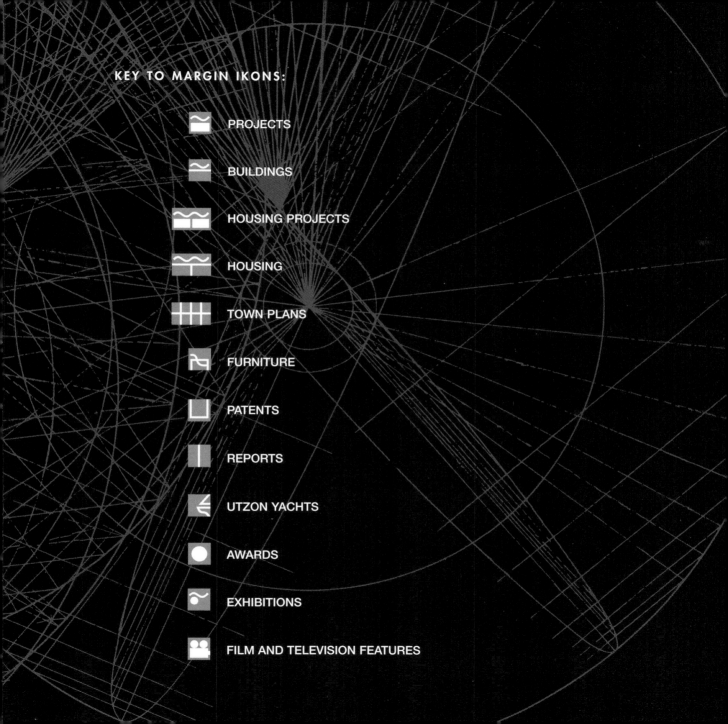

KEY TO MARGIN IKONS:

PROJECTS

BUILDINGS

HOUSING PROJECTS

HOUSING

TOWN PLANS

FURNITURE

PATENTS

REPORTS

UTZON YACHTS

AWARDS

EXHIBITIONS

FILM AND TELEVISION FEATURES

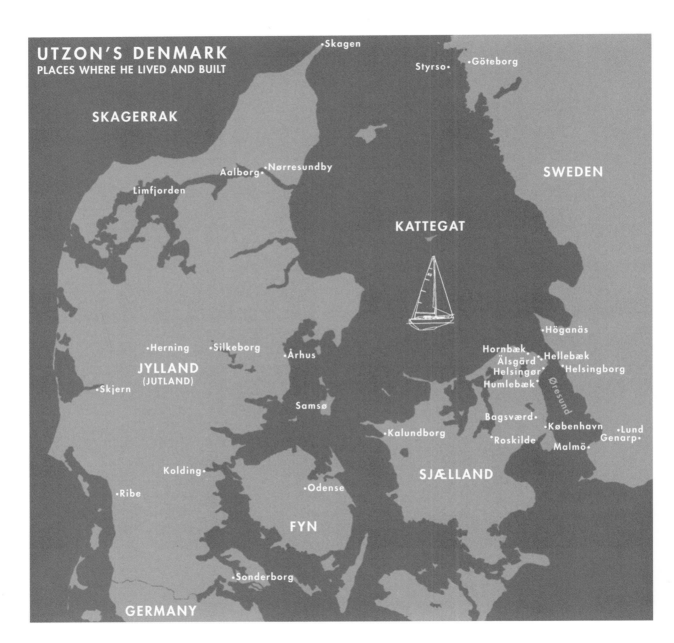

UTZON'S DENMARK
PLACES WHERE HE LIVED AND BUILT

SKAGERRAK

SKAGEN

Styrso• •Göteborg

SWEDEN

Aalborg• •Nørresundby

Limfjorden

KATTEGAT

•Herning   •Silkeborg   •Århus

JYLLAND
(JUTLAND)

•Skjern

Samsø

•Kalundborg

Höganäs•

Hornbæk•   •Hellebæk
Älsgärd• •Helsingborg
Helsingør•
Humlebæk•

Bagsværd• •København •Lund
•Roskilde   Genarp•
              Malmö•

Øresund

Kolding•

•Odense

SJÆLLAND

•Ribe

FYN

•Sonderborg

GERMANY

'By nature, I am a simple man, who loves his family, wife and children, and who does not presume to have all the answers. But it meant a lot to me to grow up around the shipyards where my father worked. Since my childhood, I have seen what man can create with tools. What exceptional forms that could be created with hand tools, and this has given me an optimistic belief that we can do many things.'

Utzon was educated at the Aalborg Katedralskole until 1937. Eldest Son of Aage Utzon and Estrid Valeska Halina (nee Olsen), Utzon grew up at Aalborg where his naval architect father Aage Utzon (b. Hellebæk 1885– d. 14 Nov. 1970) was chief engineer of the local shipyard during 1920s and 1930s. Subsequently his father moved to Helsingør as Director. Aage Utzon was a talented yacht designer who trained at Armstrong College, Newcastle, England before WW1. An example is the *Explorer* a 50 m^2 ketch. Aage Utzon developed the Aalborg dingy and supplied plans to home boat builders to encourage an enjoyment of the outdoors. Many hundreds of copies of his designs were built in Denmark and Sweden. He participated in sailing regattas on Limfjorden and on the Swedish west coast in his cutter *Shamrock* (1918–). Aage became obsessed with the traditional Danish type of double ended boat known as a *spidsgattere,* or *spitsgatters* in Norway, made famous by the Norwegian naval architect Colin Archer of Larvik (b.1832–d. 1921) in the years after 1899. He developed a series of 30, 45 and 55 m^2 *spidsgattere* boats and won many honours from foreign countries with designs in *Yachting World,* an English magazine, for his fine construction drawings. His designs were particularly appreciated on the West Coast of America particularly his ocean–going vessels of the *Sisu* and *Lene* types of blue water yachts. The Utzon family were avid yachtsmen and sailed on the long Limfjorden Sound which divides Jutland in two at Aalborg and has many bays and islands. In later years at secondary school he often visited his father's shipyard where he studied new designs, helped his father to draw up final plans for new types of yachts and made models

As a teenager, Utzon used to go with his father and friends on excursions to North Jutland. The climate there was very harsh. The summer holidays were spent at Helsingør with his grandparents in North Zealand and it was here he met two artists, the Dane **Paul Schrøder** and **Carl Kylberg** (1878–1952), from Sweden. They introduced him to art and were an important influence on his later artistic development. Kylberg lived in a house next to Utzon's grandmother. As a young man Utzon was deeply engaged with painting for many years. Kylberg was already an old man when Jørn Utzon encountered him at Ålsgårde, and later in Stockholm, where Utzon spent WW2. Utzon recalled: 'for me it was a great inspiration to speak to Carl Kylberg. He taught me about the introspection in nature that he knew so well. He constantly dealt with this theme in his work: longing and expectation. I repeat it again and again to myself, that Kylberg found a source of great wealth in his inner being, as can anyone who dares to open themselves up. There was a sense of timelessness in him like that of water and life.'

An additional influence was the Danish sculptor, **Einar Utzon–Frank** (b. 13 March 1888), a professor at the Royal Danish Academy of Fine Arts and his father's cousin.

1918

NOV 11   Armistice is signed in the forest at Compiegne ending World War I.

1923

OCT 5   Erik Oberg Utzon is born on 5 October 1923.

1929–36

Davis Hughes enrols as a student in science at University of Tasmania but fails to complete his degree and does not graduate. He obtained results in the following subjects: Education I (P), Chemistry I (P), Pure Mathematics 1b (P), Applied Mathematics (P), Physics (P); Physics 2 (P), Chemistry 2 (D), Chemistry 3a (D).

1930

Utzon's parents visit the great exhibition in Stockholm in 1930.Utzon states: *'This was the exhibition where Scandinavian functionalism had its breakthrough in the Victorianism of the time. Here they experienced the new simple white architecture that demanded light and space, that let the sun shine in and rejoiced in the functional, the unconcealed, Functionalism if you will. It was the Swedish architect Gunnar Asplund's exhibition building (Exhibition Building, 1930)… My parents returned home completely carried away by the new ideas and thoughts. They soon commenced in totally redoing our home. The concept was space and light, all of the heavy furniture was moved out and simple things were brought in. We developed new eating habits: healthy, green and lean. We began to exercise, get fresh air, cultivate light and the direct so called natural way of doing things…'*

1932

The War Memorial Opera House in San Francisco, by Arthur Brown, G. Albert Lansburg, and Willis Polk architects opens in 1932 with a capacity of 3,252 seats. During the opera season 2 rows were removed to accommodate the orchestra reducing the capacity to 3,176 seats (300 standing). It was damaged in 1989 by the Iona Prieta earthquake, and, after repairs costing US$84.5 million, it reopened in 1996.

1934–37

Asplund completes the extension of the Göteborg Law Courts. **Asplund, (Erik) Gunnar,** b. Stockholm 1885, d. Stockholm 1940.

1936

NOV 30 Crystal Palace destroyed by fire. The BBC news announced that evening: *'The Crystal Palace is no more'*.

1937

JUNE Utzon finishes school at 18 after taking examinations intended to qualify him for university.

JULY 12 The Musical Association of NSW annual report urges the establishment of a national house for opera and drama to mark the 50th anniversary of the State in 1938 at Centennial Park.

SEPT 100 candidates began training period and Utzon the last of 25 selected with Poul Schouboe to study at architecture school.

OCT 1 Utzon enrols at the Royal Akademie. His final examination marks at secondary school were poor, especially mathematics, and he failed to qualify for entry to the Polytechnic High School.

1937–42

Instead, he enters Royal Academy of Arts, Copenhagen, and studies architecture under professors **Steen Eiler Rasmussen** (b. 1898–) and **Kay Fisker** (1893–1965). In 1942 he completed his thesis and was awarded his diploma in architecture. Eiler Rasmussen wrote London: *The Unique City* in 1934, rev. ed. 1982, & *Experiencing Architecture*, 1959.

KAY FISKER

Kay Fisker b. Copenhagen 1893, died at the age of 73 in 1965. His works include: Hornbækus, Ågade, Copenhagen (1923); Århus University (Kay Fisker won competition with C.F. Møller and Povl Stegman (1931); The Museum of Natural History, Århus U (1937–39); Vestersohus with C.F. Møller (1935–39); Housing at Voldparken (1949–51); Voldpark School at Husvm (1953); Building for the Organisation Young Mothers' Assistance, Strandboulevard, Copenhagen (1954–61); Danish Academy in Rome (completed after his death in 1963).

1939

Kastrup Airport Terminal (1936–39) by Vilhelm Lauritzen (1894–1984) opened. The hall had a corrugated shell roof 12cm thickness spanning 15m.

JULY 26   Jørn Utzon submits plans for outhouse on his grandmother, Martha Olsen's, property at No. 4a nørdre strandvej 226, Ålsgårde. It is accompanied by a letter specifying all the materials to be used. Work is completed in 1940.

1940

APR 8   Jørn meets Lis at her 21st birthday party, attended also by Tobias Faber. They awake next morning on Utzon's birthday to find Denmark occupied by Germans forces.

APR 9   **German troops land at Copenhagen and Denmark surrenders under the threat of an air bombardment of the city.**

Jørn Utzon gains early office experience with **Gunnar Biilman Petersen**, the first professor of Graphic Arts at the Royal Academy.

JUNE 17   Davis Hughes claims in an application for the position of temporary education officer, Civil Staff, submitted to Royal Australian Air Force: 'I read for Bachelor of Science Degree at the Universities of Tasmania and Melbourne completing it in the following subjects…'in subsequent application forms he repeatedly claims to have a B.Sc. degree. He states he was Senior Mathematics and Chemistry Master at Caulfield Grammar School, residing at 217 Glen Eira Road, East St Kilda. S2.

JULY 6   Davis Hughes marries Joan Phillipa Johnson.

OCT 30   Death of Erik Gunnar Asplund (b. Stockholm 1885–d. Stockholm 1940)

DEC 12   Davis Hughes joins R.A.A.F. as Flying Officer (Honorary)

1941

MAY 14   **McKell government** sworn in in N.S.W. with Mr. J.J. Cahill, Minister for Transport.

SEPT 4   Davis Hughes departs Australia for U.S.A.–Canada, arrives Oct. 10, 1941. Duties escort.

OCT 14   Departs Canada Oct. 14, returns to Australia on Nov. 4, 1941.

NOV 12   Davis Hughes appointed Flying Officer, with rank of Flight Lieutenant, No. 253785 (Education).

DEC 1   Davis Hughes classified A4B fitness.

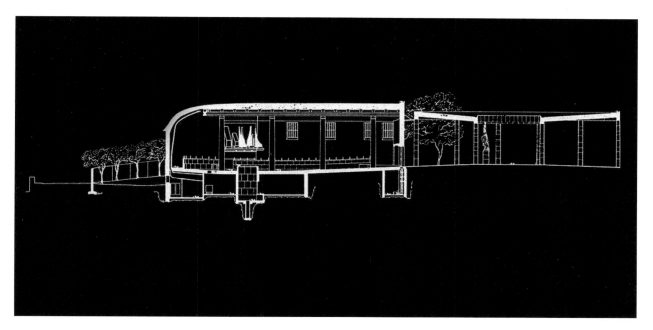

Forest crematorium chapel, section through chapel, Asplund

Ragnar Østberg's 1923 Stockholm City Hall
helped the city to rediscover its waterfont

> ## ASPLUND
>
> Asplund was one of the most significant of Swedish architects of the first half of the 20th century. His work shows the transition from traditional to modern architecture. Asplund's projects include the Skandia Cinema (1922–3), Stockholm City Library (1924–7), Stockholm Exhibition (1930) notably the Paradise Restaurant, Göteborg Law Courts Extension (1934–7), Forest Crematorium (1935–40). Alvar Aalto's obituary could equally well describe Utzon: '…everything started with people and all the innumerable strands of their emotional life, and with nature. All of Asplund's works clearly convey the same affinity with nature, including man as a part. Much could be written about Asplund's art and his various stylistic periods, but this immediate feel for nature will always be found at the bottom of it.'

1942

JUNE   Dip. Arch degree is conferred on Utzon.

JULY 2   Meeting between Jørn Utzon and Tobias Faber at Copenhagen Town Hall to discuss his departure from Denmark, leaves for Stockholm 1 or 2 days later.

JULY 4   Jørn Utzon leaves Copenhagen for Stockholm, Sweden.

SEPT 23   Tobias Faber joins Utzon in Stockholm.

DEC 4   Marries **Lis Fenger**. Lis Utzon was a commercial artist before her marriage. Utzon is 6ft 4in (194.3 cm) tall with grey–blue eyes. Both sets of parents attend wedding held in Stockholm. Gunnløgsson and wife present also. They share house with Halldor Gunnløgsson at Drottingholm (Jan.–June).

1942–45

Following the occupation of Denmark in the Second World War Utzon obtains work legally as an architect in Stockholm at the same office as Gunnløgsson. Tries to persuade Faber to go to Sweden with him. Lives with Gunnløgsson and wife in house at Osterlanddutan, Drottingholm, but problems arise and they move to Gammlastan in the old part of the city. Faber lives at Baggenstan St. Nils and Karen Clemmensens, Halldor and Celie Gunnløgsson and Jørn and Lis take their skiing holidays north of Stockholm in 1943, 1944 (April). Utzon Joins Danforce the Danish brigade training there in 1945 and subsequently spends three years as Assistant architect in office of **Professor Paul Hedquist**,

Stockholm (Folkskola i Fredhall – elementary school at Fredhall, Stockholm). Works with **Hakon Ahlberg** who wrote book, *Gunnar Asplund 1885–1940*, Stockholm. Admires Courthouse at Göteborg, the Forest Crematorium in Stockholm by Asplund. Göteborg Courthouse is an extension of an existing Town Hall.

1943

MAR 20 Train from Stockholm to Mattmar Station for March 20 to 30 holiday in Central Sweden, at Hoakenvalen Bydalen region. Party comprises Lis, Jørn, Halldor & Celie.

APR 7 Davis Hughes is involved in non–flying accident at Western Junction (near Launceston, Tasmania), while with RAAF. Hughes is cleared and no blame is attached to him.

APR 8 Lis celebrates her birthday in Stockholm flat with Tobias Faber. Jørn is away on business.

JUNE Kongelige Danske Kunstakademiets Arkitektskole is closed and activities are dispersed around Copenhagen in response to the German military occupation of the Academy building disrupting normal teaching activities.

OCT 30 Leif Oberg Utzon marries Annie Christensen (b. 11 May 1920) the daughter of the previous Manager of the Helsingør shipyard.

READINGS IN CHINESE ARCHITECTURE

While he is in Stockholm, Utzon studies Osvald Siren's books on Chinese architecture with Tobias Faber: (*Les Palais Imperiaux de Pekin*, Paris, 1926; *Tch'ang–nan au temps des Souei et des T'ang.* Revue des Arts Asiatiques, no. 1–2, Paris, 1927; *Historie des Arts anciens en Chine.* vol.IV: architecture. Van Oest, Paris & Bruxelles, 1930). In 1950 explores Taoism. Utzon's interest in Chinese architecture was stimulated by the articulation of column–and–beam. As a student at the Royal Academy, he was a friend of Else Glahn (*Scientific American*, May 1981, p. 132) who later was director of the Institute of Asian Studies at Århus University from 1974–79, following earlier studies of Chinese architecture in Japan and China.

1944

Bellahøj, Copenhagen (competition), 3rd prize Multistorey housing scheme competition for Bellahøj in Copenhagen. In these early years Utzon collaborates with Tobias Faber (b. 1915–). **Tobias Faber** writes: *'In helping him draw up the final plans, I began a close collaboration with Utzon on the first of seven or eight architectural competitions.'*

Aalborghallen (competition), honourable mention. Requirements include concert hall, theatre and meeting halls.

Danish architectural community in Stockholm, comprised Nils & Eva Koppel, Karen & Ebbe Clemmensen, Ole Holweg, Erik Asuussen, Erik Christian Sørensen (younger), Halldor Gunnløgsson, Tobias Faber.

FEB 4   Davis Hughes is appointed Squadron Leader (Acting).

MAR 29   Ski holiday, Cerie Gunnløgsson, Karen Clemmensen, Jasco, Lis, Jørn, Tobias at Hoakenvalen, Bydalen region in Central Sweden.

APR 8   Lis' birthday celebrated while skiing while staying at Hotel Dromumce.

APR 11   Ski Party returns to Stockholm

JUNE 24   **Nazis dynamite Tivoli (f. 1843) in Copenhagen on the night of June 24.** Nearly half its beloved buildings, including the music theatre were destroyed as a reprisal for resistance activities against the German Wehrmach.

JULY 1   Davis Hughes is appointed Squadron Leader (Temporary) RAAF.

1944–45

Utzon receives Gold medal of the Royal Academy of Fine Arts of Copenhagen. *'This'* he explains, *'is a kind of doctor's degree acquired by participation in an annually arranged competition by the Academy for architects under 35 years of age. In 1944 the subject was an academy of music with concert hall.'*

SEPT 27   Jan Oberg Utzon is born.

1945

Project for a crematorium.

Water tower and Sea Mark, on the island of Bornholm

Utzon graduates from the Royal Academy of Fine Arts Copenhagen and becomes a member of DAL/AA (Danske Arkitekters Landsforbund/Akademisk Arkitektforening or the Association of Architects).

MAR   Conditions of Crystal Palace competition published.

APR   Jørn Utzon in Skane in south, 2 week camp waiting to cross into Denmark with Danforce free brigade. Training camp at Tingsryd in barracks; last 2 weeks spent at Genarp where the entire Danish brigade is assembled in 8 to 10 camps. At Genarp, news received from General Montgomery that the Germans had given up Norway and Denmark.

MAY 3	Admiral Hans von Friedegurg surrenders the German forces in Denmark to Montgomery.
MAY 5	Jørn in uniform as truck driver, also Tobias. Jørn crosses the sound on 5 May, Tobias a day later, on 6 May. Not in touch with Faber. Enters Helsingør and drives south to Copenhagen. Faber continues to Jutland.
AUG 15	Jørn Utzon writes to Alvar Aalto and mentions he has a small gold medal of the Danish Academy.
SEPT	Radio Building, State Broadcasting Corporation, Rosenørns Allé, Fredericksberg, by Vilhelm Lauritzen inaugurated (1934–45). The 1,200 seat funnel shaped box Concert Hall has a 12cm (4.8in) thick concrete shell roof spanning 40 metres and suspended undulating ceiling 2.4in thick. It was lined with panel strips of maple veneer and dark Oregon pine, chairs covered with ox hide.
OCT 2	Tobias Faber moves into Utzon's flat at Rosenørns Allé 57. Lis & Jørn depart for Finland so Utzon can work in Alvar Aalto's office in Helsinki.
OCT 25	Utzon is employed at the Aalto house and office at Munkkiniemi (1934–36), Finland, until December 5, 1945. Utzon recommended by Erhard Lorenz, who had worked in the office 1938–39 and at the same time as Utzon. He spends just six weeks there and returns suddenly after receiving a letter from Copenhagen. Continues to correspond with Aalto afterwards.
DEC 10	Davis Hughes is demobilised (awarded War Medal)
DEC 11	Utzon returns from Finland. Tobias Faber and Jørn Utzon discuss possibility of going into partnership together.
DEC 12	Tobias Faber's birthday: Jørn & Lis celebrate with him.
DEC 29	Utzon works on Crystal Palace competition.

1946

	Utzon commences his own office with various factory buildings for fish–products and a chemical factory.
	Falkoping, Sweden (competition) 4th prize. Community centre, theatre.
	Borås Bebyggelsesplan, Sweden (competition) with Tobias Faber. Honourable mention. Housing.
	Architectural Association's one–family houses and town planning (competition) 1st & 2nd prize.
	Næstved Idræsarlaeg, Denmark (competition) 3rd prize. Sports centre.
	Hobro Pavilion, Denmark (competition) 4th place. Restaurant and Community centre.
MAR 10	Design begins on the Crystal Palace competition, London, with **Tobias Faber** (b. Dec. 12, 1915 son of Arne F. and Bodil (nee Johansen) married to Grete Wern) and **Mogens Irming**. Crematorium (project).
MAR 11	Utzon sends a telegram to Alvar Aalto to say he cannot go to Finland because Lis is ill.

MAR 20   Faber moves from Utzon's flat at Nr. 57 into Rosenørns Allé 58, Copenhagen, opposite. Clemmensens and Jørn help him to move on May 10–12.

APR 5   Crystal Palace competition drawings sent. Work started in Rosenørns Allé 57 because it had more space.

MAY 3   Friday: Result of Crystal Palace competition announced by Lord Ammon Chairman of the Crystal Palace Trustees at a luncheon at County Hall. Assessors: Sir Patrick Abercrombie, Dr Charles Holden, Alister Holden, Sir Kenneth Clark, Rt Hon Lewis Silkin MP. 87 designs submitted: 1st Herbert Jackson & Reginald Edmund (Birmingham); 2nd Eric Lyons & Roy Christy; 3rd Johnson & Lanchester & Lodge. Scheme Nr. 72 by Clive Entwistle + O.N. Arup (structural engineer) + J. Varming (Heating & Ventilation engineer) singled out for praise by Le Corbusier; no. 85, Faber Irming & Utzon scheme unplaced — submitted model plus drawings. Sir Kenneth Clark, the representative of the Arts Council among the assessors adds: *'The assessors have not awarded the prize to a great pioneering work or to a great masterpiece of architecture. A number of pioneer works have been submitted, but they were not workable.'* Le Corbusier remarked: *'Does the premiated scheme embody the prodigious acquisitions accumulated between the two wars? Not at all! It is pseudo–modern architecture of about 1925.'*

MAY   Eugene Goossens arrives in Brisbane.

MAY 21   Lin Oberg Utzon is born in Copenhagen.

JULY 1   T. Faber travels to Stockholm.

SEPT 8   T. Faber returns to Copenhagen from stay in Sweden.

1947

The Bissen Prize is awarded to Utzon; this enables him to undertake travel and studies in Europe and Morocco (North Africa) in 1947–48.

Århus Idrætsanlag, Denmark (competition) mention. Sports centre.

Housing development, Morocco (project)

Paper Factory, Morocco (project)

Central Railway Station, Oslo (project with Arne Korsmo). Utzon forges a close friendship with Norwegian architect **Arne Korsmo** (b. 1900. Villa at Vinderen, Oslo, 1937, also a house for three families at Vettakollen, Oslo, 1955, with Norberg–Schulz).

MAY 19   Legal proceedings brought against Davis Hughes by Maurice Kelly, Solicitor, Mitchell House, 358 Lonsdale Street, MELBOURNE.

JULY 2   Eugene Goossens tells reporters Sydney should have *'a fine concert hall for the orchestra with perfect acoustics and seating for 3 500 people, a home for an opera company and a smaller hall for chamber music.'*

SEPT 18	Utzon asks Aalto to recommend him for job with Parry, Shaw & Hepburn in USA, but Aalto refuses because he is dissatisfied with the office over Baker House, MIT. Style of correspondence is quite informal.
SEPT	Publication of joint article: Tobias Faber and Jørn Utzon, 'Tendens i Nutidens Arkitektur', *Arktitekten*, vol. 49, nos 7 + 8 + 9 (July, August, Sep) 1947, pp. 63–69, provides the clearest early statement of Utzon's design philosophy.

1947–48

'Vika' town planning for Oslo Centre, Norway. Office buildings. Development plan for the Vestre Vika area, Oslo (project with Arne Korsmo).

Cabinetmaker's competition, 2nd prize, furniture.

Cabinetmaker's competition, 1st & 2nd prize, glass.

1948

Publication of critical article in *Arkitekten*, U, 1948, p. 86–87 accusing Utzon and Faber of plagiarism and points out similarities with Albert Frey's book, *In search of a Living Architecture*, New York, 1939.

School of Commerce, Göteborg, Sweden (project with Arne Korsmo).

Housing competition for Borås in Sweden.

Planning of cement factory and factory for prefabricated elements, Morocco.

Jørn Utzon involved in the large Aalto exhibition in Copenhagen in 1948.

Utzon meets **Fernand Leger** (1881–1955) and **Le Corbusier** (1887–1965) in Paris and sees **Henri Laurens** (1885–1954), one of the first artists to adapt the Cubist style to sculpture. S.Giedion later claimed that Laurens showed Utzon *'how one builds forms in the air, and how to express suspension and ascension.'*

Erik Utzon graduates in *Realist* non–matriculation stream (vocational course 2 years shorter), then becomes a very young Nulårslev at Kronborg skovdistrict, under the wing of a forest ranger named Bobek. Spends 3 to 4 years training as a ship's carpenter (*Skibstømrer*) in Helsingør, and later returns to forestry and works with Mogens Mikkelsen at Giesgaard.

JULY 27	The Planning Scheme for the County of Cumberland is presented to J.J. Cahill, Minister for Local Government, at Town Hall, Sydney, at 8 p.m. Cahill's involvement in improving Sydney began at this time.
SEPT 22	J.J. Cahill is sworn into office, Minister for Works and Local Government and Deputy Premier of NSW.
OCT 7	Goossens suggests new music centre should be *'Like the San Francisco War Memorial Opera House, it must furnish a permanent home for our symphony orchestra, opera, ballet, and choral works.'*

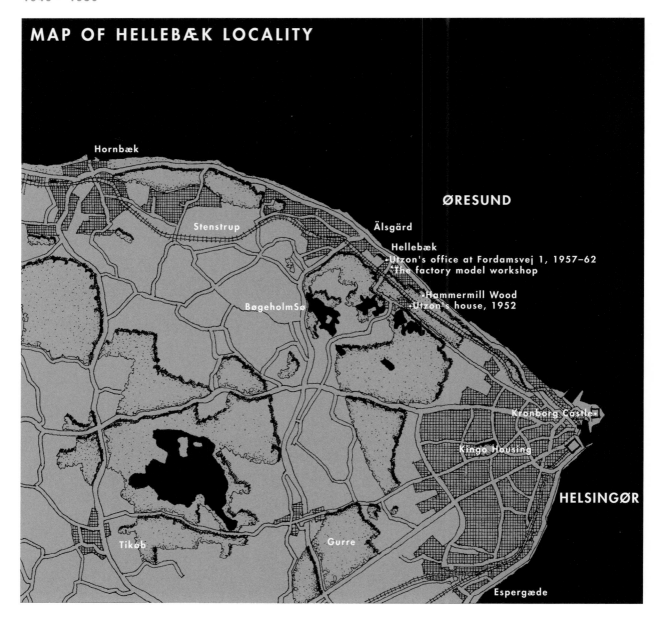

MAP OF HELLEBÆK LOCALITY

Hornbæk

ØRESUND

Stenstrup

Älsgärd

Hellebæk
•Utzon's office at Fordamsvej 1, 1957–62
•The factory model workshop

BøgeholmSø

•Hammermill Wood
•Utzon's house, 1952

Kronborg Castle•

Kingo Housing

HELSINGØR

Tikøb

Gurre

Espergæde

1949

The Zacharia Jacobsen Award funds Utzon's study trip to Mexico to look at Mayan and Aztec architecture, in the United States, and visits Taliesin East. He spends a short time with Frank Lloyd Wright in Taliesin East. Evidently, Utzon saw Eero Saarinen at his Ann Arbor office outside Chicago on this visit because in January 1957 in Sydney, he described Utzon to Ashworth: *'Utzon is a man about 42 or 44 years old. I met him several years ago — well he is a tall very handsome Dane with blond hair, as most Danes have. I've seen several competition drawings which he has won and there is a very fine quality about his work. I think you can be very happy that this project (SOH) goes in the hands of this man. I've always considered him as one of the really most talented men in Scandinavia.'* Also saw Mies van der Rohe. Visits to Monte Alban, Oaxaca, in Sierra Madre del Sur, Mexico (f. 500 A.D. by Zapotec people), and Uxmal and Chichen–Itza (f. 600 A.D. by Itza people), Yucatan. On his return, he enters numerous competitions, showing most interest in the problems to be solved rather than their formal requirements.

1945–49

Charles and Ray Eames House, Case Study House #8, Pacific Palisades, California.

1946–50

Mies van der Rohe, Farnsworth House, Fox River, Illinois USA, completed and influences Utzon's design of his own house two years later.

APR 17 Eugene Goossens proposes an auditorium with adjustable walls for Sydney.

1950

1950–1962 Chemical Factory in Copenhagen

Utzon begins in private practice in Copenhagen and works in association with brothers **Erik and Henry Andersson** who have an established office at Helsingborg, Sweden. The partnership with Andersson brothers was established in 1952. Erik Andersson (b.1914–), studied architecture at Göteborg. He was the son, grandson, and great–grandson, and great–great–grandson, in a long line of Swedish master builders and lived in nearby Helsingborg.

> ## DRUMMOND
> Drummond was minister for education in the Bavin ministry 1927–30, and again in the Stevens–Bruxner and Mair–Bruxner Coalition from 1932–1941. Drummond was responsible for the establishment of the Armidale Teachers' College on Nov. 2, 1929, the first in Australia.

FEB 11 Davis Hughes is elected the Member for Armidale replacing **D.H. Drummond** (1890–1965) who resigned his seat in 1949. Davis Hughes resided at 87 Brown Street, Armidale in 1950. He claimed the degree of Bachelor of Science in List of Members of L.A. in vol. 188, p. viii (Oct. 19, 1948–May 9, 1950).

FEB 19 Opera House now becomes an *idee fixe* with Eugene Goossens.

MAR 16 Hughes gives speech on overcrowding at the Dorrigo District Hospital. At first, he was left of centre but quickly moved to the right. His major speech is on 'Education in Rural Districts,' *(Hansard*, vol. 188, p. 5518).

1951

JAN 11 **Estrid Halina Utzon** (JU's mother) dies at the age of 57 and is buried in Hellebæk churchyard. The name 'Halina' is of Baltic (Polish) origin.

FEB Utzon now living at Kistvej 51, Hornbæk.

Utzon designs his own house, Morrocco.

FEB 1 First scheme for Utzon's own house at parcel 2bz, Hellebækgaard, Hellebæk submitted to Teknisk Forvaltning, Helsingør (Ref. 5087–50). Utzon gives his address as Kistvej 51, Hornbæk. This is the scheme which, with a few minor changes, is built.

SEPT 15 Second scheme for Utzon's house is submitted. It has a Wrightian cruciform plan and spreading horizontal roof overhangs. Utzon's address is now given as 216 nordre Strandvej 216, Ålsgårde, near his grandmother's house.

1952

APR **Utzon House**, is completed at Hellebæk, North Zealand, with open plan. An annex was added later in 1958.

In partnership with Arne Korsmo, Utzon prepares a development plan for the Skøyen–Oppsal area, Oslo.

APR 3 **J.J. Cahill becomes Premier of NSW.**

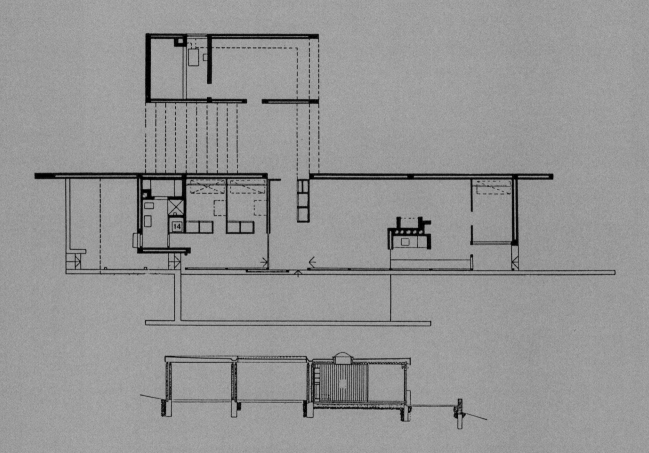

Plan and section of Utzon's house

1952–53 **House, near Lake Furesø, Holte,** a NW suburb of Copenhagen; its inspiration is partly Japanese (T. Faber).

Villa Arnung, Nærum.

1953

 House, Præstevanget 15, Hillerød. Built in 1953, high roof inside, unpublished, with some characteristic details. Later changes due to rot in woodwork.

 In collaboration with Ib Molgelvang, Utzon wins 1st prize in the: skanske hustype, Skaanske low–cost housing competition for 'Scania house types'. This is a new type of family housing in Skåne ((Skåne or Scania was previously an ancient Danish province, and once played a very important role. It is Sweden's southernmost province, and Malmo is its chief city). The competition requirements emphasised that the houses should be suitable for the outskirts of the town. Utzon based his ideas on his experience as a teenager living on the outskirts of Aalborg where his family home had a nursery garden at the front, and all the neighbours gardens contained a variety of sheds, shelters, and huts, to accommodate a wide range of activities. The Skane housing also resembled the west Jutland traditional Danish farm–house type with four wings enclosing a central courtyard. Utzon's scheme utilised a L–shaped wall, 15 m x 15 m long, placed side by side, in an irregular pattern such as he had seen done in his studies of ancient Chinese architecture. These discoveries were later employed in courtyard schemes for the Kingo Houses at Helsingør and Bakkedraget in Fredensborg. A high proportion of Utzon's competition activity targeted south–western Sweden and Oslo in Norway.

 Langelinie Pavilion, Copenhagen (competition), Utzon awarded 4th prize. Restaurant and yacht club facilities.

Skanse gardhouse.

Erik Oberg Utzon is educated at Silkeborg – Stenderup – Giesegaard Skovdistrikt; later completes his *skovfogeteksaman* (1953) in the Vejle Kommune Skovdistrikt. Excellent result.

1954

 In an open inter–Scandinavian competition for one–family–housing + town planning, Scanian types of house, Utzon is awarded 1st prize.

 Villa 1, Rungsted.

Villa 2, Rungsted (family house).

~	**1954–60**	Elineburg Housing Estate, Denmark (competition): awarded 2nd & 4th places in first stage; 1st prize final stage. The programme called for housing and town plan for 1,200 flats, flats, schools, shopping centre, subsequently realised with E. and H. Andersson.
⌐		Marieburg, Stockholm (competition), 1st prize. Administration centre + 1,000 flats.
~		Invited competition Lund (north of Malmo in Sweden), housing – 60 one–family houses, 1st prize.
	MAR 28	Proposal by **Mr Eugene Goossens** (1893–1962, left Australia in 1956) Sunday night that an Opera House be built between George and Carrington Streets, over Carrington Lane, sited over Wynyard Ramp, to cost at least £750,000 with accommodation for 3,500 to 4,000 people, and an orchestra pit accommodating from 90 to 100 musicians.
	MAR 31	Wed: design for an opera house on Bennelong Point by 5th year architecture students at University of Sydney under the guidance of H. Ingham Ashworth and George Molnar, lecturer.
	SEPT	A group of businessmen led by H.C. Coombs, governor of the Reserve Bank, in 1954 launch a campaign to establish an Australian Elizabethan Theatre Trust, commemorating the queen's visit. The Trust was funded partly by the federal government and partly by private donation. It brought Hugh Hunt from Britain as its first director and purchased an old theatre in Newtown, Sydney, which it renamed the Elizabethan. At the outset, the Trust set up national ballet, opera and theatre companies.
	NOV 18	Mr Cahill announces he has invited Lord Mayor, Ald. Pat Hills, to confer on the Government's proposal to build an Opera House.
	NOV 30	**Representative Conference is held at the Public Library with Premier present at which the constitution of the Opera House Committee is announced. 21 sites were investigated, and, from these Bennelong Point was ultimately selected.**
	DEC 7	The Committee meets for first time to select a site.
	DEC 12	Announcement that the NSW Parliament is to have new home.
		By the end of December, 1955, the competition conditions have been drafted and the Government, as promoters of the competition, approve them. W.R Laurie and Kelvin Robertson, Sydney architects, advise in the drafting of the Conditions of the competition.

1955

~	**JAN–MAR**	**21 Row houses, 21–59 Ostervag, Skjern,** south–west Jutland, (collaboration with Bent Alstrup).

≈ **Villa Frank, Vedbæk,** north–east Zealand, with Bent Alstrup.

≈ **Villa Lillesoe, Fureso.**

FEB 12 Erik Oberg Utzon, Jørn's younger brother, dies in Morocco, North Africa.

MAY 13 The Committee recommends to the Premier that Bennelong Point is the outstandingly suitable site.

JUNE Eugene Goossens is knighted at Buckingham Palace for his services to music in Australia.

JULY 27 Opera House Committee discusses the future course to be followed with J.J.. Cahill, and they agree... for the holding of an International Architectural Competition for the design of a 'National Opera House' at Bennelong Point.

OCT 14 Pier Luigi Nervi presents a paper at Joint meeting of the Institution of Structural Engineers, the Cement and Concrete Association, at Friends Meeting House, London. Ove Arup is present.

DEC 7 **Competition for SOH is announced.**

1956

≈ **Villa Dalsgard, Holte,** North Zealand.

Hans Scharoun designs a scheme for the Philharmonic Hall in Berlin, later completed in 1963. Scharoun works from models in an atelier adjacent to the building site just as Antonio Gaudi had done at the Sagrada Familia church in Barcelona.

FEB 15 Competition programme is released.

FEB 24 Eugene Goossens inspects opera houses at Vienna and Hamburg and praises the modern stage lifts provided at the Vienna State Opera House in a report to Opera House Executive Committee (OHEC).

MAR 8 The NSW Police vice squad brief their colleagues in Customs and suggest senior Federal officers be at Mascot airport to meet the Qantas flight carrying Goossens to question him about letters and photographs which had previously been liberated from Rosaleen Norton's King's Cross flat in Brougham Street and which implicated him in their sex magic rituals.

MAR 9 Friday morning, 8 a.m.: arriving on a flight from London, Sir Eugene Goossens is asked if he has anything to declare and he replies *'No, no, Nothing.'* Goossens had concealed the materials in folders of heavy paper, sealed with adhesive tape and bearing on the outside the names of composers, presumably with the object that they should be taken as containing sheets of musical scores. Goossens is interrogated over 6 hours and is arrested and later charged at the Bathurst Street police headquarters for being in possession of pornographic material.

MAR 15	Closing date for registration in the *National Opera House competition*, Sydney. A deposit of £A10 is required. *Brown book*. It was expected there would be about 200 registrations, but 933 competitors register, 721 of whom proceed further and obtain conditions.
MAR 18	Goossens submits formal letters of resignation from his positions at both the ABC and the NSW State Conservatorium.
MAR 22	Four days later, Sir Eugene Goossens pleads guilty and is fined £100 for having imported prohibited goods in his possession. He is temporarily relieved of his duties.
MAR 26	Saturday: Goossens slips out of Mascot on a KLM flight to Rome travelling incognito as Mr. E. Gray on his 63rd birthday.
APR 9	Jørn Utzon celebrates his 38th birthday.
MAY	Utzon begins work on SOH competition entry and completes a scheme in his spare time in December 1956.
MAY 3	Federal ALP Executive decides to refer NSW Labour faction dispute for decision by special conference in Melbourne on June 11.
MAY 15	Questions from competitors.
JUNE 1	Answers to competitor's questions are posted.
JULY 21	The Australian Elizabethan Theatre Trust launches the Elizabethan Opera Company with a national production of *The Marriage of Figaro* (1956), at the Theatre Royal, Adelaide with Robert Quentin, general manager, Stephen Haag, production manager, Joseph Post, musical director.
	Knud W. Jensen approaches Utzon to design the Louisiana Art Museum at Humlebæk soon after Christmas 1955 Utzon says, 'I don't have time.' Wilhelm Wohlert recommended instead early 1957, and with Jørgen Bo, the pair completed Lousiana museum in 1958. Jensen's three wives were all called Louise and the highly successful museum which developed from the original modest family house is named after them.
SEPT 11	State Cabinet gives its approval for the removal of 150 ft height limit on Sydney city buildings.
OCT	Utzon is invited by UNESCO in New York to accept a post in Egypt planning rural communities in the Valley of the Nile.
DEC 3	Closing date for competition submissions: assessed in approximately 2 weeks; publication of the award within 8 weeks from the date of closing of the competition.

COMPETITION JURORS

All four judges were architects, none had theatre, opera or musical acoustic expertise and there was no representative of the client. During the judging they held a guessing competition on the nationality of contestants and Martin was convinced Utzon was an Englishman. Saarinen observed of the result: 'I would like to add this: during the judging of the competition, many times we said that this was really the work of a genius, and were very impressed with the result. And now what is better proof for a competition being a success than that the first prize is a really great scheme.'

Cobden Parkes (b. Balmain 1892–), Sir Leslie Martin (b. Manchester 1908–2000), Eero Saarinen (b. Kirkonummi, Finland 1910, d. Ann Arbor, Michigan 1961), Ingham Ashworth (b. Manchester 1907, d. Sydney 1991 aged 84).

1957

JAN 1 Tuesday: Kim Oberg Utzon, born on New Year's Day.

JAN 7 Monday: commencement of adjudication; 3 judges begin work and take ten days to make their choice. Ashworth later insisted that Saarinen arrived one-and-a-half days late [Saarinen actually arrived four-and-a-half days late] and, by which time, Utzon's scheme had already been picked out with other contenders.

JAN 7 Eero Saarinen and wife Aline lv. Detroit on AMERICAN Flt. 231 at 11.40 a.m.

JAN 11 Friday: Eero Saarinen lv. Nandi (Suva) PAN AMERICAN Flt 843 lv 1.00 a.m. and arr. 7.30 a.m. in Sydney, Australia. Stays at HOTEL AUSTRALIA, in Sydney. Saarinen walks to Bennelong Point first on his way to NSW Art Gallery.

JAN 12 Saturday night: Qantas hangar at Mascot by architects Rudder Littlemore and Rudder collapses. The roof was 345 x 150 ft (105 x 45.7m) and weighed 100 tons (99,792kg).

JAN 13 Sunday morning: Saarinen and Martin visit Palm Beach.

JAN 16 Wednesday: Professor Martin and Mr. Saarinen are guests at a civic reception given by the Lord Mayor, Alderman H.F. Jensen. The judges worked morning, afternoon and night and completed their deliberations by Jan 18.

JAN 18 Friday: The four judges hand in their report and their selection to Mr. Stanley Haviland, chairman of the Opera House Committee at an informal ceremony in the Lands Department Building. Martin and Saarinen leave Sydney on the weekend.

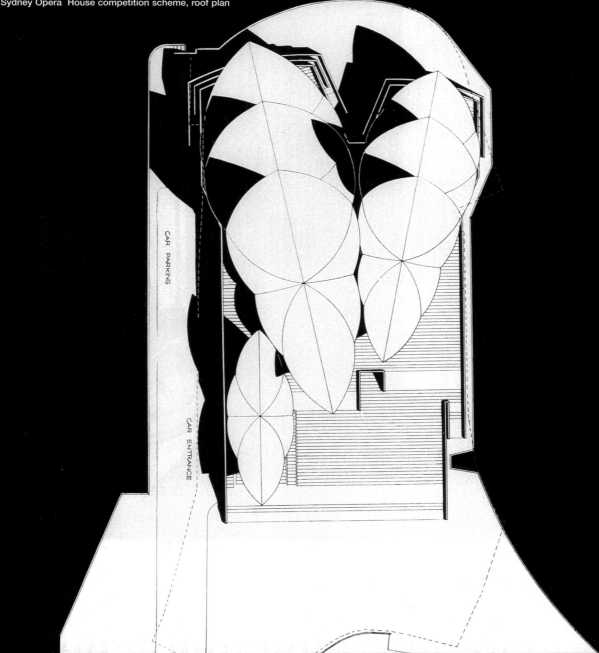

CAR PARKING

CAR ENTRANCE

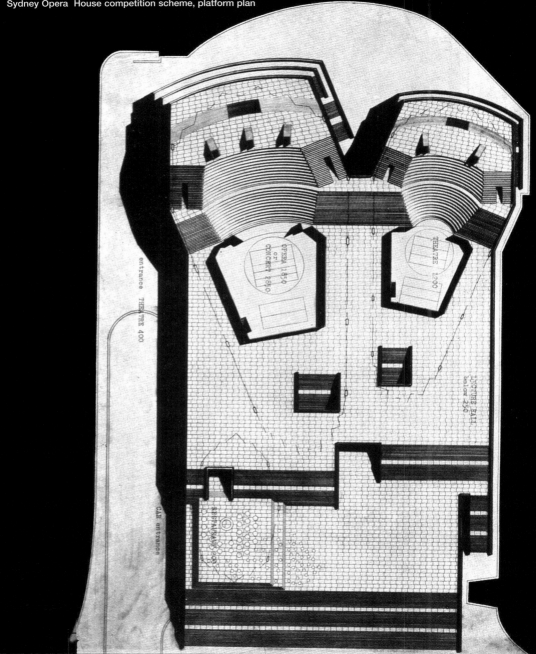

JAN 19	Sat: Eero Saarinen and Aline visit Walter R. Bunning at his Mosman home in the morning before they depart by air for Djakarta (Indonesia) on QANTAS Flt EM 551 lv. 10.00 p.m. Return trip via Jogjakarta, Bandung, Djakarta, Singapore, Ceylon, Bombay, Aurangabas, Bombay, Ahmedabad, Karachi, Istanbul, Rome, arr. London Thur. Jan 31, 3.30 p.m. where Aline and Aero separate, she to return to New York.
JAN 21	Monday: Aged 66, Mr Cahill's retirement is in sight, but problems over the choice of a successor cause its postponement.
JAN 24	Thursday: after the competition result is announced, because there was some doubt whether the project would proceed, at Aline Saarinen's suggestion, Ashworth makes a long recording with Martin and Saarinen, and Saarinen's slow speech is speeded up. It was in the form of a question and answer with the questions put by Ashworth and Martin and Saarinen giving the answers about the competition. Copies of the 3 records are sent to the 3 participants and the original is deposited with ABC Historical Library (now Radio Archives at ABC Ultimo Centre in Harris Street).
JAN 29	Australia, Tuesday 3 p.m: the result is announced at the Art Gallery of NSW. Mr Cahill begins talking at 3.15 p.m. opens envelope at 3.29 p.m. to announce that scheme 218 is the winner.
	Sydney Opera House (competition) 1st prize. Utzon collaborated with Erik Andersson but Utzon became the dominant designer and the entry was submitted in his name.
	Denmark, Tuesday night: Utzon speaks to *SMH* reporter from his home at Hellebæk by radiotelephone.

PARKES

Cobden Parkes was the son of Sir Henry Parkes and was born Balmain in 1892. He joined the Public Service as a cadet draughtsman in 1909, during WW1 served with the First AIF in Egypt and Gallipoli. In 1935 appointed Government Architect held this position until 1958, acting as officer–in–charge of building and planning at UNSW. He was awarded the Gold Medal of the RAIA in 1964.

MARTIN

Martin was a year younger than H.I. Ashworth, and, like him was born and educated in Manchester and studied architecture at the University School of Architecture, 1926– 30. He recieved his doctorate in 1934, and from 1956–72 was professor and head of the Department of Architecture at the University of Cambridge. With Sir Robert Matthew, Peter Moro and Edwin Williams at the London County Council (1949–56), he designed the Royal Festival Hall, London (1951). In 1967, Martin was invited, with three others, under the chairmanship of Shaikh Jaber Al–Ahmed, Kuwait's Prime Minister, to advise on the new city of Kuwait. Among his most important recommendations in 1970 were Arne Jacobsen for the Central Bank commission and Utzon for the Parliament Building. See *Architecture, Education and Research,* Academy Press, London.

JAN 30 Wednesday. night: Spokesman for Opera House Committee announces that a public appeal would be launched within the next two months for funds to help build the £3,500,000 National Opera House.

FEB 3 Sunday: It is announced that Utzon will be required to pass an examination set by NSW Architects Registration Board.

Ove Arup writes to Utzon after reading competition result in *The Times*, London, to offer his services as consultant.

FEB 5 Tuesday: Utzon flies to London from Copenhagen to meet Leslie Martin and Eero Saarinen to discuss the way the Opera House project should be carried out. Martin recommends that Utzon be given personal responsibility for developing the program but should have technical support for the problem of calculating and later building the complicated concrete shell vaults by working with a firm such as Ove Arup and Partners. Professor Martin and Mr Saarinen introduce Utzon to Ove Arup during his stay in London. The UNITED STATES EMBASSY BUILDING (1955–1960), designed by Saarinen was under construction at Grosvenor Square, London. Saarinen was selected for the project on Feb. 19, 1956.

FEB 7 Thursay: Saarinen lvs. London on SCANDINAVIAN Flt. SK 522, at 1.10 p.m. arr. Oslo (Norway) 6.25 p.m. Stays at GRAND HOTEL (US Embassy Building project).

FEB 9 Saturday: Saarinen lvs. Oslo on SCANDINAVIAN Flt. SK 905 at 8.50 p.m. arr. N.Y. Sun., Feb. 10, 9.50 a.m., and arr. Detroit on CAPITAL Flt 25 at 2.50 p.m.

FEB 11 Monday: Utzon commissions model maker to prepare 1 : 200 model for Opera House Executive Committee (OHEC).

ARUP

Ove Nyquist Arup (b. Newcastle–upon–Tyne 16 April, 1895, d. Highgate, 5 Feb, 1988) was educated at Preparatory School, Hamburg, and Sorø Public School, Denmark. He was a year behind the Danish modern pioneer Vilhelm Lauritzen (b. 1894–84) at Sorø Academy, and studied philosophy and mathematics at the University of Copenhagen, completing his BA in 1916, before studying civil engineering at Royal Technical College, Copenhagen, 1916–22, m Ruth Sørensen in 1925. He joined Christiani & Nielsen, Hamburg, as a designer in 1922, transferred to their London office where he remained till 1934. From 1934 to 1938 he was Director and Chief Designer of Messers J.L. Krier & Co, which he left to found Arup Designs Ltd and Arup & Arup. In 1946 he started Ove N Arup, Consulting Engineers, which became Ove Arup & Partners in 1949. He worked with Lubetkin to produce Highpoint, the Penguin Pool and Finsbury Health Centre, where he applied new ideas of concrete construction, namely, the use of load–bearing concrete walls. The Rubber Factory at Brynmawr, 1951, with the Architects' Co–Partnership, was the first postwar building to command world attention, especially for its ingenious roofing of 7.5cm thick concrete domes over a series of nine bays. The 107m span Kingsgate Footbridge at Durham, built in two halves and completed in 1963, was fittingly his last project as it encapsulated his ideal structural synthesis of economy and a highly original method of construction. In the Opera House drama, Arup played Polonius to Utzon's Hamlet, who expostulating endlessly seeks 'By indirections [to] find directions out.' He invariably injected a philosophical openness into each search for engineering economy.

FEB 28 Ashworth writes to Utzon stating his preference for Ove Arup and Partners, London, as the project's consulting engineer.

MAR 1 Cahill calls for £500 million to be spent on housing.

MAR 4 At Saarinen's suggestion, Utzon undertakes a study tour of five totally new opera houses and concert halls in Europe to examine their details and sizes of secondary rooms.

MAR 7 Mr Askin asks, *'Is the present the right time to push ahead with this desirable but lavish venture?'*, and *'How does the Government propose to finance it?'*

MAR 21 Utzon refers to two models and agrees to work with Ove Arup.

APR 2 Cahill suggests that four lotteries be held every year, each with a £50,000 prize and tickets at 30 shillings until opera house paid for. This would raise about £240,000 annually. Mr. Morton (Liberal), Leader of the State Opposition, called the plan repugnant.

APR 17   Model of SOH is completed. Utzon expresses concern that it is rather big and very fragile, warns that the gilt underside of the shells must under no circumstances be touched.

APR 27   Saturday: Cahill tells the annual conference of the women's ALP organising Committee, *'We are anxious to build this opera house if we can. We have to be prudent, keep our balance and have regard to the views of the people.'* Cahill casts doubts on whether the OH will go ahead. A substantial section of NSW state Caucus is firmly opposed to it.

APR 29   Sunday: Cahill says Opera House should be built in addition to more homes and urges that a public appeal for funds be launched.

MAY 8   Caucus votes 24 to 17 to approve the launching of public appeal and early construction of OH. Mr. J. Seiffert (Monaro) gives notice of a recision motion. The voting shocked Cahill, as it indicated a hopeless split over the issue.

MAY 9   Cahill faces a crisis over the issue and announces he will take no further action until the annual conference of the NSW Party on June 15.

JUNE 5   Motion to rescind approval of construction is withdrawn.

JUNE 6   *'No split says Cahill'*.

JUNE 8,9   A meeting of the Australian Labor Party on weekend of June 8 & 9 approves Opera House project.

JUNE 11   Utzon sends set of photographs of the model to Cahill, Premier of NSW.

JUNE 16   Sunday: majority approval for the go ahead on the Opera House on the voice vote is unmistakable. The victory is due to Cahill's earnest advocacy a day earlier on Saturday June 15. Cahill's hand considerably strengthened by the State ALP decision.

JUNE 18   Assessors recommend Ove Arup be appointed consulting engineer.

JUNE 19   Sir Bernard Heinze and Jørn Utzon send congratulations to Cahill.

JUNE 24   Ove Arup sees Utzon and looks at other work he has done; he forms best opinion of his ability as an architect.

JULY 3   State Parliamentary Labor Caucus votes overwhelmingly in favour of building Sydney's Opera House. Mr Cahill assures Caucus that no State Loan funds would be used to finance construction.

JULY 10   Wednesday: Utzon sends model of Opera House by air carrier to OH Executive Committee, Sydney. Advises he will arr. Sydney, Saturday 14 July, at 5 p.m. On about July 10, Ove Arup, Jenkins, Mr Ahm and Mr. Mollman come and spend a week with Utzon at Hellebæk.

JULY 17   Saarinen writes to Ashworth recommending a selection for acoustic consultants. Leslie Martin writes a long letter to Ashworth on acoustic design and consultants.

JULY 29	Monday: Utzon arrives in Sydney for the first time accompanied by **Erik Andersson** aboard a Lockheed Constellation L749. Met by Danish Consul General, **Mr F. Henning Hergel**. Utzon travels to Sydney via USA stopping at Los Angeles to see Neutra who expressed the hope the SOH would be built.
AUG 1	Thursday: Utzon and Andersson unpack model in the basement of the Town Hall preparatory to exhibiting it in the vestibule for launch of appeal for funds. Model is 4ft long and 2 ft 6 in wide (1.22 x .76m).
AUG 2	Friday: Utzon and Andersson visit Bennelong Point and are interviewed by **Gavin Souter** (a *SMH* journalist).
AUG 7	Wednesday: 2.30 p.m., Opera House appeal launched at a public meeting in the Sydney Town Hall to raise £1 million ($2 M). Utzon addresses the meeting. £235,500 raised in just one hour before an enthusiastic crowd of 2,500 people. Hammond sells kisses. Utzon pays £50 each to kiss Miss Shaffer and Mrs Ricci. Kisses raised £295/15/. 'Seven women' and 100 men form Sydney Opera Appeal Fund Committee.
	The Opera House Committee now becomes the Sydney Opera House Executive Committee (SOHEC) and two advisory panels are established to advise the Executive Committee: Technical Advisory Panel (TAP) with Ashworth as chairman, and the Music and Drama Advisory Panel (M & DAP) with Bernard Heinze as Convenor.
AUG 12	Wednesday: Utzon and Andersson study for a NSW Board of Architects' examination to be allowed to work in NSW as architects, missing an opera evening, and is coached by local architects.
AUG 16	Utzon has his first meeting with the Executive Committee. He is given the two Advisory Panel's recommendations for priorities of usage and sizes of the two halls and is asked to submit complete sketch plans and elevations within six months.
AUG 18	Sunday 7.15 p.m. on 2FC. Jørn Utzon Guest of Honour broadcast on ABC radio.
AUG 22	Thursday: Utzon lvs. Sydney. Before his departure, Utzon announces on Wed, 21 Aug., after a 3 week stay in Sydney, that the SOH foundation stone will be laid in 18 months time. Promises to return in February 1958 with a set of large drawings of SOH. Final technical drawings are to be completed by February 1959.
	Utzon flies back to Denmark by way of Japan and USA taking more than 4 weeks on the return leg. Visits Kunio Maekawa's office in Yotusya, Tokyo. Studies temples and sees Wright's Imperial Hotel in Tokyo. In the United States he visits theatres, concert halls and inspects Minoru Yamasaki's reception halls for the airport at St Louis (1953–55) which consist of a series of intersecting barrel vaults; sees Mies van der Rohe in Chicago and visits his new IIT school; after Chicago he meets Saarinen on Tues., Sep 17, 1957, outside Detroit; next, in New York, he later inspects the Seagram Tower and holds discussions with experts on shell–vault construction.

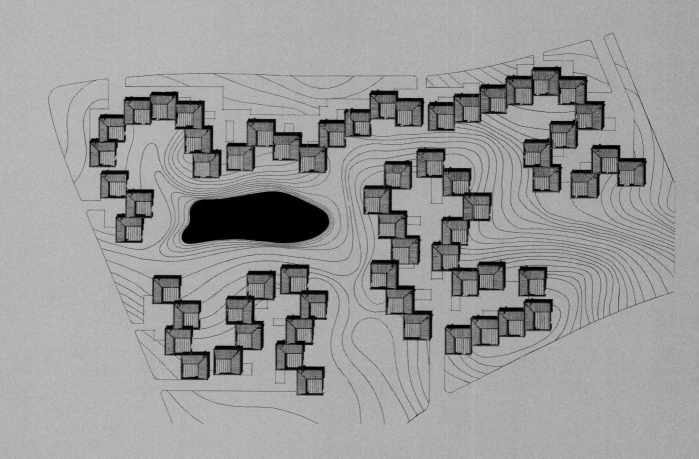

Kingohusene Housing Estate plan

AUG 31	Publicity Committee of the Sydney Opera House Appeal Fund discusses weekly collections of 3d and 6d among householders to raise money.
SEPT 7	**Hartvig Petersen & Booth** from Utzon's office travel to Vienna and inspect The State Opera and Burgtheatre there and the Festival Hall in Salzburg.
SEPT 17	A Note in the Calendar of the Eero Saarinen & Associates office at Birmingham, Michigan, 25 km NW of Detroit, reads: 'Mr. Utzon here at 12 noon.' Saarinen was working intensively on the TWA Terminal project at New York's Kennedy Airport and discussed developments and studies his model; Utzon mentions seeing the 1 : 10 models.
OCT 4	**First artificial satellite *Sputnik 1* put into orbit at an altitude 946 kilometres and a velocity of more than 28,565 km/hr. Utzon was impressed and remarked: *"It goes up and never comes down."***
	Stefan Haag, Executive Director of the Australian Elizabethan Theatre Trust, Sydney's fledgling operatic society, is appointed to the SOHEC.
NOV 8	SOHEC instructs Utzon to provide for a reduced audience of 2,800 for concerts and an audience for opera of not less than 1,700 and not more than 2,000.
NOV 11	Letter of engagement sent to Utzon by NSW government.
1957–60	**Kingohusene Housing Estate, near Helsingør, Denmark.** 63 Kingo–houses; the client is the Mayor of Helsingør.
	The Eckersberg Medal is awarded to Utzon.

1958

	Arup and Utzon in Sydney at beginning of the year.
	Workers' High School, Højstrup, Denmark. Project.
	High School sheme at Hellebæk near Helsingør. 3rd prize.
	Labour Organisation College at Helsingør, First Prize in competition. Utzon is unable to proceed because of his commitments to Sydney Opera House project, subsequently, the job was given to and is completed by **Ebbe & Karen Clemmensen** with **Jarl Heger** (1967–69).
	Melli Bank, Teheran, Iran. Modelled skylights formed by stepped parallel beams span the width of the banking hall rather like musical notation. A similar motif was later applied to Bagsværd Church in 1968. Its builder was Kampsax A/S, a Danish company.
JAN 2	Utzon is paid A£5,000 pounds by NSW government.

FEB 24   Jørn Utzon registers with the Board of Architects of NSW (cert. no. 1861).

FEB 25   Utzon is paid £10,000 by NSW government.

Yuzo Mikami leaves Tokyo for Brussels, sent by K. Maekawa as site supervisor for Japanese Pavilion at Brussels Expo 1958.

MAR 26   Utzon arrives for second visit to Sydney and presents *Sydney National Opera House* document, the '*Red Book*' (65 x 40 cm). QS prepare an estimate of £4,812,000. Seating capacity: 2,702 for concerts, 1,826 for opera. Approximate volume of Major Hall: 1,100,000 c.ft. for concert, 650,000 c.ft. for opera. R.T.: 1.8–2.0 sec. for concerts, 1.6–1.8 sec. for opera. Max width seating area: 120 ft (36.6m), length 180 ft for concerts, 115 ft for opera. Two–way parabolic roof scheme persisted till April 1961.

MAR 31   Utzon and Arup are interviewed by the Premier who asks that the work be commenced in February, 1959. To permit an early start, the job is divided into three stages: Stage 1 – platform, Stage 2 – roof vaults, tiling, Stage 3 – walls & interiors.

APR 9   Wednesday: meeting between Jørn Utzon and Ove Arup in Ashworth's room at the School of architecture at Sydney University at 3.30 p.m., introduced to Mr J. Rankin, City Building Surveyor. Discussion between Utzon, Moses and Hunt, after which it is announced that the big hall is to have a maximum of 2,800 for concerts and 1,700 for opera, with no balconies, and Utzon agrees to add a 400–seat experimental theatre inside the podium.

On return trip to Denmark, Utzon visits Peking and studies beautiful staircases there and floating roofs of temples, later sends Ashworth a copy of 900 year old Chinese building code. At this time no work had been done on the structure, on the heating or services, and no one knew what stage technique would be required. The sketch design was materially altered and documents requested before Christmas with work to start in early 1959.

S. Giedion states that after 1957 Utzon, found opportunities to visit China, Nepal, India, and Japan. In Peking he met Professor Liang who made a collection of ancient Chinese building laws from before 800 AD and had translated them into modern Chinese in seven volumes. Visits Yun Kang caves near Tatung, west of Peking in China.

APRIL 11   SOHEC Meeting: decides to let the Stage I contract before working drawings…and notes disadvantage in terms of a definite price for the contract. Closing of tenders set for Jan 19, 1959. Quantity surveyor makes new estimate of £4,880,000.

APR 17   **Expo '58 Brussels opens.**

**APR 26 –
MAY 11**   Kunio Maekawa visits opera houses in Germany and Austria with Mikami for his Ueno Hall, Tokyo.

MAY 21   Maekawa returns to Tokyo. Shows Mikami letter from Utzon asking Maekawa for a young assistant from Brussels to work in his office. Mikami agrees.

APR 28   **Bent Alstrup** submits plans to the Teknisk kontor, Espergærd, for a second north pavilion behind Utzon's 1952 house at Hellebækgaard, Hellebæk, consisting of a long drawing office and guest bedrooms linked by a glazed gallery to the dining area.

MAY 2   Utzon asks Erik Kolle to make a model of folded slabs available to **Mr. Ralph Symonds** about construction of formwork. Symonds writes to Ashworth, 12 May 1958, promising that a form, light and rigid, can be supplied with plastic surface unbroken for length of 50 ft from his new hot press (50' x 6' wide).

MAY 6   Davis Hughes (Armidale) is elected Leader of the NSW Country Party, with Charles Benjamin Cutler (Orange) as his Deputy. Voting in a secret ballot of the 15 C.P. MLA's upon retirement of M.F. Bruxner, 76, Hughes defeated Cutler for the Leadership and Cutler was then appointed deputy leader unopposed. In April 1959 Cutler replaced Hughes as leader (1959–1975), and William Adolphus Chaffey (Tamworth) elected Deputy under Cutler (1959–68).

MAY 12   Engineers of the Sydney Maritime Services Board sink test bores on Bennelong Point and in the water, seeking bedrock.

JULY 2   Mr S. Haviland, chairman of Executive Committee announces the April 9 meeting changes to the press, and states the Opera House will be finished by June 1962 (in 4 years).

JULY 4   Charles Moses asks Utzon for his opinion on which of the 3 main halls would be most suitable for use by the SSO for radio broadcasts.

JULY 7   Mikami arrives in Copenhagen via London. Meets Utzon at his Hellebæk house with Ove Arup, Ronald Jenkins & Povl Ahm of OA & P. Starts work 8 July. Draws elevations of base without roof at 1/16 = 1'0". Utzon's office at this time consists of Knud Lautrup–Larsen, Aage Hartvig Petersen, Mogens Prip–Buus, Charlotte la Cour (furniture designer) and Gerda Corydon (personal secretary).

JULY 9   Shell geometry refined and 1/5" = 1'–0" scale model built.

JULY 15   Utzon replies to Charles Moses suggesting the Main Hall be used for ABC radio broadcasts.

JULY 17   Utzon to Ashworth, mentions that *'Mr Arup and some of his staff have been here in Hellebæk for some time, and I have been one week in London.'* Arup to Ashworth, states he has just spent a week with Utzon in Hellebæk with Mr Jenkins, Mr Ahm and Mr Mollman from his office.

AUG 6   Waagner–Biro invites Utzon to Vienna to experience the Vienna operatic season.

AUG 13   Meeting of the Technical Advisory Panel, chaired by Ashworth, considers large scale drawings submitted by Utzon and Report (17 July 1958).

AUG 16   Eero Saarinen and family make a trip to Europe during which they make a stop–over in Copenhagen on Saturday, 16 Aug. Aline continues journey, but Eero breaks his trip, and does not leave until Sunday morning, 17 Aug., thus, he could have spoken to or met Utzon on the Saturday afternoon or evening. Saarinen's notes to his secretary only discuss itinerary and hotel preferences and make no mention of seeing Utzon. Saarinen was greatly taken by Utzon's work.

AUG 18   First phase of construction begins with the demolition of the Fort Macquarie tram shed on Bennelong Point by contractors Johnmann Constructions Pty Ltd for £894 ($1788).

AUG 25   Utzon is paid £5,000 by NSW government.

SEPT 2   Utzon has just returned from the Brussels World Exhibition where he saw Kunio Maekawa's pavilion which he says is '*both strong and quiet.*'

SEPT 10   Utzon is paid £28,120 by NSW government.

SEPT 20   Utzon: 'For several weeks we have had two of Arup's people in our office Mr Mollman and Mr Ahm to decide the final system for the structures.'

SEPT 24   Vilhelm Lassen Jordan gives Utzon the volumes and reverberation times figures for Major Hall 1,200,000 c. ft., 1.8–2.0 sec; Minor Hall 270,000 c. ft., 1.3–1.6 sec.

SEPT 26   **Helge Hjertholm** (Norway) joins the office.

OCT   THE OCTOBER SCHEME submitted late in 1958. In a response to criticism, he introduces a separate balcony at the rear of the halls. Seating capacity: 2,800 concerts; 1,833 opera. Volume of Major Hall: 920,000 c. ft., 630,000 c. ft. opera; Dimensions: width 116 ft. concerts; length 170 ft. concerts, 100 ft. opera.

OCT 6–10   Mikami goes to OA & P London office for liaison, meets Ronald Hobbs, Bob Kelman, Ted Happold, Peter Rice, Edward Perry and others.

OCT 18   The Lord Mayor of Sydney, Harry Jensen (Dec1, 56 – Dec 1, 65), announces that since 17 July the public appeal for funds has been a failure with $960 received, costs of salaries and stationary amounting to $1,456.

OCT 23   Thursday: Utzon leaves Hellebæk for Sydney and takes his 'October Scheme' with him containing a complete set of plans, sections, & elevations of the sub–structure. Shells drawn but only schematically. No SOH drawing numbers issued at this time.

OCT 26   Sunday: Utzon in New York to meet Wilder Green, Assistant Director, Department of Architecture at the Museum of Modern Art.

NOV 3   Monday: Utzon in Sydney calls tenders for SOH Stage I. Ove Arups represented by R.S. Jenkins, with Mr Varming and Mr Balslev present. In November, preliminary designs made of auditoria, stage towers, glass walls.

NOV 14	Tender documents for Stage I issued to 6 firms, based on Schedule of Rates and Provisional quantities.
NOV 26	Ove Arup & Partners, Structural Engineers, formally engaged.
DEC 5	Utzon leaves Sydney and stops off in India.
DEC 8	Dansk Patent No. 90550 Postringselement, issued 5 March 1961 published, 29 May 1961. The idea is a failure.

1959

Birkehøj — project for a small town to be built in North Zealand, Denmark.

Davis Huges moves to 85 Brown Street from 87, Armidale.

JAN	SOH 5 setting out of measurement drawing by Mikami.
JAN 2	Hugo Molman, OA & P's engineer–in–charge of shells visits Hellebæk office.
JAN 7–12	Mikami draws intersections of shells in parabolic profile for exhibition at Museum of Modern Art, New York.
JAN 19	Tenders close for Stage I: Civil and Civic lowest at £1,397,878 ($2,795,756) compared to Hornibrook £1,616,060 ($3,23,120), and the highest bid, McDonald Constructions, with £2,227,781 ($4,455,562).
JAN 21	Rider & Hunt supply new SOH cost estimate to Utzon of £5,300,000, an increase of £420,000 from the previous April 11, 1958, estimate.
JAN 23–28	Mikami designs *Inaugural Plaque* for the commencement ceremony, & screwdriver for J. Cahill.
JAN 29	R.S. Jenkins (OA &P) visits Sydney to examine tenders in conjunction with Quantity Surveyors and recommends acceptance of Civil & civic Contractors.
JAN 30	**Davis Hughes, Leader of NSW Country Party, announces a seven–point policy program in the run up to the March 1959 election.**
FEB	*Four New Buildings: Architecture and Imagery*, exhibition opens at Museum of Modern Art on the Sydney Opera House, curated by Wilder Green. Features: National Opera House Sydney, Australia by Jørn Utzon; Notre Dame de Royan, France by Guillaume Gillet; First Presbyterian Church Stamford, Connecticut, by Harrison and Abramovitz; and Trans–World Airlines Terminal Idlewild Airport, New York, by Eero Saarinen & Associates.
FEB 4	State Cabinet accepts the lowest tender from Civil and Civic Contractors Pty Ltd of NSW, managed by Gerardus Josef (Dick) Dusseldorp (b. 1918–d. Tahiti 2000). Civil & Civic was formed in 1951 to carry out a housing project for the Snowy Mountains Authority. Work commences on the site.
FEB 14	*Inaugural Plaque* completed at Helsingør Shipyard in great haste.

1959

FEB 18	Utzon & Lis leave for Sydney carrying *Inaugural Plaque* with them. <u>Utzon is paid £23,655 by NSW goverment, taking total amount to £71,775.</u>
FEB 18	Meeting at Utzon's Hellebæk office on Feb. 21, he is seen by Hugh Hunt on SOHEC (Executive Director Australian Elizabethan Theatre Trust) on a visit to Copenhagen to check architect's drawings of stage technique; includes trips to Malmö and Göteborg Municipal theatres.
FEB 23	Utzon stays at Reef Hotel, Honolulu, Hawaii.
FEB 25	Wednesday: Davis Hughes to deliver Country Party policy speech at Armidale Town Hall on 4 March. Around this time, Davis Hughes is admitted to The Prince Alfred Hospital in Sydney after suffering a nervous breakdown.
FEB 27	Friday: Utzon arr. Sydney at 21.55 p.m. on Flt. BA 708 with Lis for short stay and brings bronze plate. Booked at Hotel Astra, Bondi Beach, Sydney. Entertained by Ashworth and wife Ella, meets children, Lis Utzon is entertained by Mrs Winston and Towndrow who take her on a tour of northern beaches real estate. They also spend time with Arthur and Elspeth Baldwinson, Max and Jean Collard at Palm and Whale Beaches.
MAR 2	Monday 2.30 p.m. ceremony to celebrate the commencement of work on Bennelong Point. Work starts on Stage I of SOH. Charles Cutler (Orange), Deputy Leader of NSW Country Party, gives speech supporting SOH project. **Olaf Skipper Nielsen** a Danish architect, is appointed as Utzon's site representative. Stays in Sydney until 1963. In the *Gold Book*, Utzon comments: *'Even one building may make a difference to a city. In 1920 the city of Stockholm commissioned an architect [Ragnar Östberg] to design a new city hall [1909–23]. From the day the building was finished the face of the city began to change.*
	For the architect had seen the soul of Stockholm and turned the people's minds to the beauty of the waterfront and the possibility of improvement. When architects work they try to express the climate and the personalities of the people who will live and use a house. The architect must be inspired.
	I am sure the people of Sydney will understand when I say how deeply I feel my responsibility and how much I am inspired by it.'
	Hellebæk Office telegrams Jørn, 'are celebrating the day in sunshine with Inaugural cake and champagne. Congratulations, office, family and friends.' The party was held at the Red House office, 1 Fordsvej, with the children of staff attending and a full size cake decorated exactly as the *Inaugural Plaque* designed by Mikami.
	NSW Leader of the Opposition, Mr P.H. Morton offers to abolish land tax, road maintenance tax, increase number of school bursaries, complete Sandy Hollow railway, overcome Sydney sewerage in five years, overcome housing shortage in three years. Cahill costs promises at £343 million.

MAR 3   Meeting of the Technical Panel is attended by Utzon and Arup.

MAR 4   Wednesday: NSW Premier, Mr Cahill takes plan for the Commonwealth to establish a national housing corporation with additional capital of £25 million to the Special Premiers' Conference in Canberra.

MAR 4   Wednesday: Mr C.B. Cutler, Deputy Leader delivers Country Party policy speech on behalf of Davis Hughes at C.P. Election launch. Mr. P.H. Morton Leader of Liberal Party speaks in support. Party Officials deny rumours Davis Hughes is about to retire because of ill–health. Mr. Cutler to take over only for the duration of the election campaign.

Statement by Mr Percy G. Love (Labor Party candidate) and Mayor of Armidale, speaking at Bundara, says that he was, *'really surprised at the extent of feeling against Mr Hughes in the Armidale electorate.'*

MAR 11   In Commonwealth Parliament, Mr Griffiths (Shortland) questions the Minister for Air, Mr Osborn, about checks on Davis Hughes claim of B.Sc. degree in RAAF List of Feb. 1942 (Flt Lieutenant), Oct. 1944, and May 1945 (Squadron Leader), and later employment at the Armidale School on basis of the List.

MAR 13   Country Party officials deny rumours that Mr Davis Hughes had resigned the Party Leadership.

Jørn and Lis Utzon leave Sydney at night by BOAC airliner.

MAR 20   Friday: it is claimed Davis Hughes is the subject of a smear campaign.

MAR 21   Saturday: the State votes.

MAR 22   Marked swing to Liberal and Country Party, Government in danger of defeat. Result on Sunday morning: Australian Labor Party, 43 seats, Liberal–Country Party 44, 6 seats in doubt. The swing against the Government most marked in the country. *Sun–Herald*: 'The only country seat in which the Opposition on early figures appeared to face a threat was Armidale. But on later figures, it seemed that the Country Party Leader, Mr Davis Hughes, would retain his seat.'

MAR 25   Announcement that Davis Hughes has been warned by his medical advisers against carrying on as Country Party Leader.

MAR 28   Jørn and Lis Utzon in Teheran, Iran, extend their stay till Saturday 4 April.

MAR 29   Sunday: Davis Hughes leaves Gloucester House, Royal Prince Alfred Hospital, Missenden Road, Sydney. Official explanation is he is suffering from a stomach ailment and nervous exhaustion. Goes on holiday to Newport on North Shore to recuperate.

MAR 31   Tuesday: Mr Cahill names the new Cabinet. ALP result: 49 seats.

APR 1   Frederiksberg town plan, Denmark (competition) Utzon is awarded 1st prize; he is notified by telegram in Teheran. Frederiksberg is close to Copenhagen.

APR 1–9   Mikami visits OA & P office, London.

APR 3	Saturday night: Davis Hughes returns to Armidale.
APR 6	Davis Hughes returns to electoral duties in Armidale.
APR 13	Lobbying for Country Party posts begins.
APR 14	Tuesday: Davis Hughes relinquishes leadership of NSW Country Party. Mr C.B. Cutler, MLA for Orange, is elected as the new Leader.
APR 20	P. Ahm, R. Kelman & others visit Hellebæk.
APR 21	Tuesday: Davis Hughes makes a statement in the NSW Legislative Assembly in response to an accusation which arose during the election campaign that he falsely claimed to have a Bachelor of Science degree from the University of Tasmania in which he conceded he misled the Parliament about his university qualifications and also had falsely claimed to hold a B. Sc. degree in June 1940 while enlisting in the Royal Australian Air Force.
APR 24	Visit by Utzon and Mikami is followed by meeting at Vilhelm–Jordan laboratory at Gevinge, where 1 : 10 scale acoustical model of Major Hall with stepped parallel walls is being tested. Jordan shows his model and explains his acoustic work.
APR 30	Lis Utzon thanks Mrs Winston: *'I hope we shall be able to make up for this when we come to live in Sydney.'*
MAY 23	Perspex model of the shells at 1 : 60 scale delivered from Helsingør Shipyard.
JUNE 8–9	Shell roof model affixed to wood model of base superstructure.
JUNE 10	Dr. Walter Unruh, German Stage Technique consultant, visits Utzon at his Hellebæk office.
JUNE 15	Utzon travels in Scandinavia.
JUNE 15–19	Wood model of stepped design for Major Hall auditorium is assembled.
JUNE 19	Utzon: *'we have been terribly busy and have almost continuously people from London or people from my office in London.'*
JUNE 22–27	Ove Arup, P. Ahm, R. Kelman visit Hell. office, discuss double shell structure, stage towers, etc.
JUNE 24–25	Utzon goes to Paris for meeting with Le Corbusier.
JULY	**Robert Askin replaces Morton as the Leader of the NSW Parliamentary Opposition and begins to revitalise the Liberal Party Opposition.**
JULY 27	Mikami begins work on the design of Minor Hall Auditorium based on a sketch by Utzon inspired by waves breaking.
AUG 10–14	Minor Hall drawings for 1 : 60 model finished showing radiating sections.
AUG	**Libby and Peter Hall** marry in London where they were both working; they later visit Hellebæk on their honeymoon and meet Jørn Utzon and Yuzo Mikami. They attend a party given by Utzon.

AUG 20   Kunio Maekawa & wife visit Denmark, meet Utzon, T. Faber, H. Gunnløgsson, E.C. Sørensen, Palle Svenson & others.

AUG 27   1 : 60 scale model of Minor Hall auditorium made at Helsingør Shipyard, arrives. Looks very promising. Utzon photographs model resting on Yuzo's head.

AUG 30   Osmond Raymond Jarvis (RAIA, A 1946, F 1958) arrives at Hellebæk, works on documentation.

SEPT   Jørn Utzon and Prip–Buus invited to Vienna by the Austrian engineering firm Waagner–Biro to experience the Viennese operatic season first hand. They inspect the mechanical stage facilities of the Burgtheatre (opened 1748), formerly Theatre bei der Hofburg, it was the imperial court theatre of the Hapsburgs and was destroyed by fire in 1943, rebuilt and reopened on Nov. 5, 1955, after being refitted with an electrically driven revolving stage containing vertical stage lifts. Utzon wrote to W–B with thanks on Sep. 29, 1959, mentioning the drawings he had taken away of the Salzburg theatre and the revolving tower from Vienna.

Concrete outline drawings of substructure prepared, including concourse beams. During Sep–Oct, preliminary study made of the Major Hall Auditorium and its use for various purposes (Jørn — Aage — Yuzo).

SEPT 5   Prof. Yoshikatsu Tsuboi, Kenzo Tange's structural engineer visits Hellebæk.

SEPT 11   Utzon photographed with a model of the Melli Bank, Teheran.

OCT 6   Utzon sends 1 case of drawings and photographs to Museum of Modern Art for exhibition on SOH.

OCT 13–15   Suggestion of placing the orchestra podium in the middle of the Major Hall is examined.

OCT 20   Hugo Mollmann visits Hellebæk office. Discussions held on shell columns.

OCT 22   Joseph Cahill is taken ill at a Caucus meeting in Parliament House, refused to be taken next door to Sydney Hospital and is driven into the hospital yard instead in his official car. Dies of complications resulting from a gastric ulcer.

OCT 28   **Robert James Heffron (b.Thames NZ 1890–1980) becomes Premier of NSW on death of J.J. Cahill the following week.**

OCT 30   Dr. V. Jordan visits Hellebæk office: discussion of acoustics.

NOV–DEC   Uses of Major Hall Auditorium compiled in a small booklet for the client. Jacob Kielland–Brandt joins the office.

NOV 6   Payment of a further £20,000 authorised bringing total payment to date to £91,775.

NOV 16   Ralph Symonds officially opens its new factory at Homebush Bay.

DEC 10   Utzon refers to Knud Lautrup–Larsen as his right–hand man in the office. Set of drawings of the stage area in the Major Hall completed. Lautrup–Larsen visits Sydney in early 1960 and mentions working in Sydney.

1960

Publication of **Helmer–Peterson**, Keld, 'Jørn Utzon: A New Personality', *Zodiac no. 5* (1959), pp. 70–105.

Pavilions complex, World's Fair, International Exhibition Centre in Copenhagen (project).

National Museum, Copenhagen (competition project)

Elvira, Spain (competition) for a Mediterranean town.

Eliveberge Housing, Sweden. Scheme for a shopping centre.

JAN   Utzon is asked to prepare drawings for a parking arrangement for 1,100 cars and proposes to form a parking garage within the rock formation fronting the southern end of the Opera House site where an underground car park is eventually built in March 1993.

JAN 5   R. Jenkins, R. Kelman (OA & P) visit Utzon's office.

JAN 6   They are joined next day by O. Arup, H. Mollmann.

JAN 11   Utzon writes to **Mr. George Nelson,** a critic for Herman Miller, about furniture designs for SOH and asks whether it can be produced by Herman Miller Furniture and mentions talking with his friend Charles Eames.

JAN 12   Dr Walther Unruh, consultant for stage technique, arrives.

JAN 15   Utzon leaves for Sydney.

JAN 21   Thursday afternoon: Jørn Utzon in Sydney to inspect progress at Bennelong site and to discuss new and detailed plans for seating and stage layout. He reveals the 'roof will be made of netted wire and sprayed with reinforced concrete and later tiled.'

JAN 26   Tuesday: Official site inspection.

FEB 1   Knud Vodder (furniture designer) joins the Hellebæk office.

FEB 5   Friday: after 8 days, Utzon departs from Mascot for San Francisco. Promises to return in Dec.1960 or Jan. 1961.

FEB 4   **James Thomas** (U.K. architect) joins the office.

FEB 15   Utzon back in Denmark from Sydney trip.

FEB   Start made on detailed drawings at ¼" = 1' 0" scale, including finishes.

FEB 19   Jørn discusses the principle of interior finishes with Yuzo Mikami and others.

FEB 22–24   Utzon discusses the design of Major Hall interior with Yuzo Mikami.

MAR   R. Kelman (OA & P) visits to discuss + 30 ft level design of the Minor Hall stage.

MAR 6   Utzon sends 1/16" scale drawings and includes a copy of *Zodiac 5* to Ashworth.

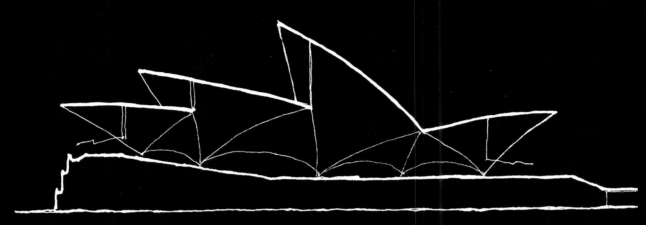

Competition scheme (A), 1957: freehand, single skin r.c. shell

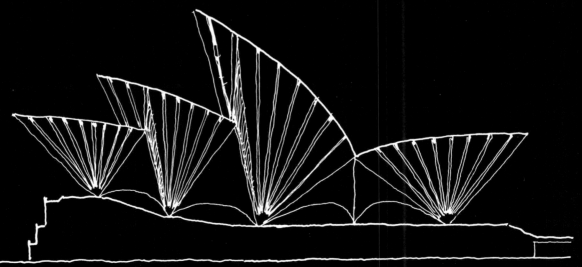

Early parabolic scheme, Feb. 1958 (B): parabolic ridge and rib profile, single skin r.c. shell with ribs

MAR 7–8	Prof. Unruh visits office to discuss stage technique.
MAR 8	**R.S. Jenkins** and Associate **H. Mollman** from Arups' office visit Hellebæk to study problems with the stage areas. Goddard, Peak & Mason of Rider & Hunt (quantity surveyor), visit.
MAR 14–16	Discussion with Utzon on stage tower walls, louvre plane of the shells.
MAR 22	Jørn and Lis invite Yuzo Mikami to dinner to celebrate his birthday.
	First Reading of the *Sydney Opera House Bill* introduced into State Parliament by Mr Heffron; bill is attacked by R.W. Askin.
MAR 25	Dansk Patent No. 93100 Mobel, *navnlig stol eller bord, med sarg or ben*, issued March 26, 1962, published June 18, 1962.
MAR 29	Utzon is made an associate of RAIA, NSW Chapter.
MAR 30	Ronald Jenkins (OA & P) visits office, states that structural calculations by computer for the roof shells are only approximate, and he has more hope for the model tests. Suggests use pin–point support under the shell supports to point load column head.
MAR 31	Hugo Mollmann joins the discussion.
APR 1	Dr. W.L. Jordan joins discussion.
APR 4	Hr. Rauch of M.A.N. (stage technique) arrives.
APR 5	Prof. Unruh participates in stage technique discussion.
APR 5	*Sydney Opera House Act, 1960*, second reading debate. Askin, Chaffey, Davis Hughes speak in the debate.
APR 6	Discussion with Utzon on concourse beams lasts till April 7.
APR 19	*The Sydney Opera House Act*, is assented to in the NSW Legislative Assembly, the Minister for Public Works named as the constructing authority, and an expenditure of £4,880,000 is authorised. P.N. Ryan becomes constructing authority and replaces the Sydney Opera House Executive Committee with responsibility for the project on behalf of the NSW government.
APR 28–29	New sketch from OA & P of concourse beam support; discussion by telephone between Utzon and Jenkins.
MAY 12–20	Preliminary design of louvre planes so they act as structural connecting elements to stabilise the shell complex.
MAY 23–25	Discussions with Ove Arup on auditorium balcony structure and canopy over the entrance to the experimental theatre.
JUNE 6–7	Re–arrangement of concourse steps to place the *Inaugural Plaque* in the middle of the first landing (SOH 57); shell column positions for Restaurant shells fixed.

JUNE 20	R. Kelman returns to London after long stay at Hellebæk.
JUNE 26	Start of summer holiday. Yuzo Mikami visits Germany and Greece.
JUNE 27	Utzon closes office for the summer holidays (until 16 July) and spends the holidays at Strömstad, Bohuslan, on the far northern part of the west coast of Sweden at the entrance of Oslo fjord.
	International Union of Architects (UIA) Conference is held in London. P.L. Nervi criticises architects who design structures without a proper understanding of the technical aspects viz., Sydney Opera House.
AUG 3	Utzon proposes continuous balcony seating instead of separate balconies.
AUG 4	Tender opened for Stage Technique, Lighting etc. Telegram from Sydney reads: *'Situation serious.'* M.A.N. (German) tender for stage machinery is 2.5 times more than expected and this led to the change to Waagner–Biro (Austria). Lighting and other tenders were satisfactory.
AUG 5	Minor Hall Auditorium 1 : 12 model roughly finished in workshop. Result, a *'marvellous space'*; the work is done by Vodder & Lundberg from drawings by Mikami.
AUG 8	Plywood flexible geometry units for lining corridor hallways proposed by Yuzo Mikami after discussion with Utzon.
AUG 11–19	Sketch design & small model made of Major Hall auditorium with radiating lines from two centre points.
AUG 16	Ove Arup visits office and asks Mikami to work for him in London, mainly on the Durham University footbridge.
AUG 17	Wednesday: Prof Ingham Ashworth departs Sydney on a 5 week world tour of opera houses: Covent Garden, Paris, Vienna, Salzburg, Malmö (Sweden) and the Metropolitan in New York (Aug 17–Sep 21).
AUG 22	Monday: Ashworth inspects Metropolitan Opera House, New York and visits offices of Syska & Hennessy, consulting engineers.
AUG 23	Tuesday: Ashworth arr. London.
AUG 24	Major Hall: new crystalline triangular faceted ceiling scheme introduced immediately prior to Ashworth visit to Hellebæk office, still in early development stage at the time of the visit.
	Wednesday: Meeting in Ove Arup's office, London. Present: Ashworth, Jørn Utzon and Mr Poul Schouboe, Ove Arup, R.S. Jenkins, R.N. Kelman, H. Mollman (part time). Ashworth refers to Opera House Act of Parliament appointment of the Ministry of Public Works to control the building; authorization limiting its cost to £4.8 million; scheduling of Stage II contract and appointment of a contractor for stage machinery; Stage II to commence on 1 Oct 1961; control of mechanical services and Utzon's scheme for car parking undercutting Government House.

Parabolic scheme, Dec 1960 (C): parabolic ridge and rib profile, double skin r.c. shell with two–way ribs and structural louvre wall

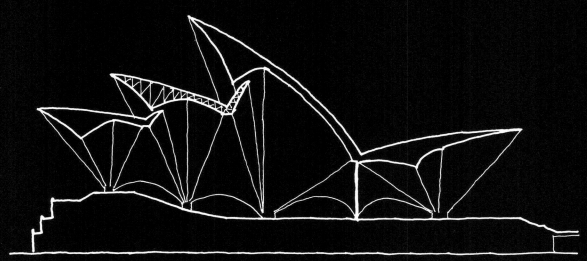

Circular arc rib scheme, April 1961 (D): parabolic ridge and circular arc rib profile, steel spaceframe with r.c. skin, louvre shell replacing louvre wall

AUG 25   **The 1960 Olympic Games open on 25 August in Rome.** Focus of world attention on the spectacular structures of Nervi, notably his big Olympic Sports Palace with its dome consisted of 144 hollow ribs illuminated by neon tube lights installed inside the hollow sections of the ribs.

AUG 25   Thursday: Meeting at Arup's London Office in morning; visit to Royal Opera House, Covent Garden. Utzon is accompanied by Schouboe.

AUG 26   Friday: Ashworth, Utzon & Schouboe visit Royal Festival Hall. New idea for Bar Area steps, to be full–width instead of narrow stairs. Folding continues from hall to lower lounge floor. Mikami telephones Utzon about the idea and Utzon immediately approves it.

Great rush to prepare models of Major & Minor Halls, shells, corridors etc in time for visit by Prof. Ashworth in the model shop.

AUG 27   Saturday: Utzon and Schouboe visit Coliseum Theatre, St Martin's Lane, London.

AUG 28   Sunday: Dep. London arr. Mannheim, Germany.

AUG 29   Monday: Utzon and Schouboe visit Mannheim Theatre, later meeting with Ashworth at Hotel Mannheimer Hof, return to Mannheim Theatre.

AUG 30   Tuesday: morning meeting Utzon & Fischer; visit Mannheim Theatre with Ashworth and Schouboe, Tronjer. Meet at Hotel Mannheimer Hof.

NERVI

Large Sports Palace, Rome, designed by P.L. Nervi based on general plan drawn up by M. Piacentini for the 1960 Olympic Games, capacity of 16,000 spectators, roof of 330 ft diameter. The dome was constructed of precast units V–shaped in section, closed by a $3\frac{1}{2}$ in (8.9 cm) thick top slab which was also precast. The whole forms a hyperstatic system in which the dome acts either as a membrane or a series of ribs each able to withstand external forces. Such a ribbed dome is very similar to the ribbed shell solution Ove Arup proposed in 1960, especially the V–shaped profile.

AUG 31   Wednesday: dep Mannheim arr. Vienna. At Waagner Biro office Ashworth, Utzon, Schouboe meet Klinger, Stroh, Wallner, Wiess.

SEPT 1   Thursday: Ashworth, Utzon + Schouboe visit Burgtheatre, Vienna, meet Teubner, Nordegg, Stroh, Weiss; return to Waagner Biro offices; and that night attend Wagner's 'Reingold' at Vienna State Opera.

SEPT 2	Friday: Ashworth, Utzon and Schouboe visit Vienna State Opera meet Sneider, Teubner, Stroh; visit Burgtheatre and attend Ferdinand Raimund's (b. Vienna 1779–d. 1836) 'Moisasurs Zauberfluch', 1827, (music by Riotte) the same evening.
SEPT 3	Saturday: dep. Vienna arr. Salzburg. Visit Salzburg Festival Hall. Meet Klinger, Weiss.
SEPT 4	Sunday: dep. Salzburg arr. Hellebæk, Denmark.
SEPT 5	Monday: Ashworth arrives in Hellebæk. Welcome party at the Utzon house followed by meeting in Utzon's office, including all members of office, and visit to model shop next door by Ashworth, Utzon and all the staff to inspect exhibition of models.
	Letter of termination sent to Balslev & Partners (Copenhagen electrical services engineering consultant).
SEPT 6	Tuesday: meeting with Ashworth, Prof Unruh, Utzon, Poul Schouboe, A. Hartvig Petersen; inspection of model shop; group visit to Louisiana Art Gallery, Tivoli Concert Hall, Copenhagen, by Ashworth, Osmond Jarvis, James Thomas and Yuzo Mikami. Later meet Prof Walter Unruh and Mr. V. Jordan.
SEPT 7	Wednesday: Danish Television films Utzon's model shop to illustrate form finding process.
	The Danish people express pride in Utzon — he has become something of a national hero. Ashworth, Unruh and Utzon present.
	Meeting at Utzon's office with Ashworth, Prof Walter Unruh, Utzon, Poul Schouboe, A. Hartvig–Petersen plus Goddard, Mason from Rider Hunt; Ashworth, Utzon, Mikami and others attend Royal Opera House performance of 'Wozzek'.
SEPT 8	Thursday: visit to Broadcasting House, Copenhagen, by Ashworth, Unruh, Jordan, Utzon, Poul Schouboe, and Mr Yuzo Mikami from Utzon's office.
	Lunch at Langelinie Pavilion attended by Ashworth, Unruh, Utzon, Poul Schouboe & Mikami; photographs taken of occasion by Utzon and Mikami; shopping at Den Permanente. Ashworth leaves from Kastrup Airport, Copenhagen.
SEPT 10	Saturday: Ashworth at Lindfield, Sussex meets Goddard (Rider & Hunt).
SEPT 10	UIA Conference members from London visit Hellebæk and Utzon explains SOH design and later gives a party at his house; Kunio Maekawa is one those present.
SEPT 13	Tuesday: Ashworth visits Sir Leslie Martin at Cambridge.
SEPT 14	Wednesday: Ashworth visits University of Southampton meets Mr Jenkins (OA &P) and inspects testing carried out on concrete shells.
SEPT 15	Thursday: Ashworth at Ove Arup's London office all day, meets Jenkins and Poul Schouboe from Utzon office and Mason (R H & P).

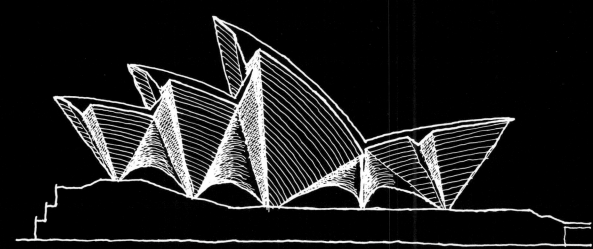

Ellipsoid scheme, June 1961 (G): elliptical ridge and rib profile, steel spaceframe with r.c. skin

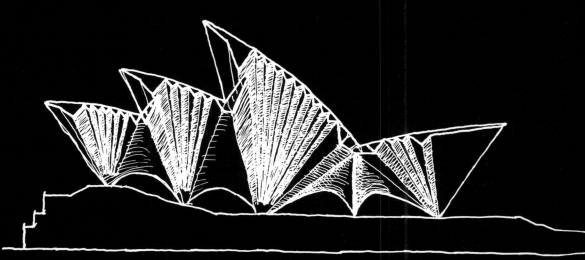

Ellipsoid scheme, Sep 1961 (H): elliptical ridge and rib profile, insitu & precast r.c

Ellipsoid scheme, Oct 1961 (J): elliptical ridge and rib profile, insitu & precast r.c

Spherical scheme, Oct 1961 (K): small circle ridge, great circle rib profile, precast r.c. ribs, structural stage tower walls

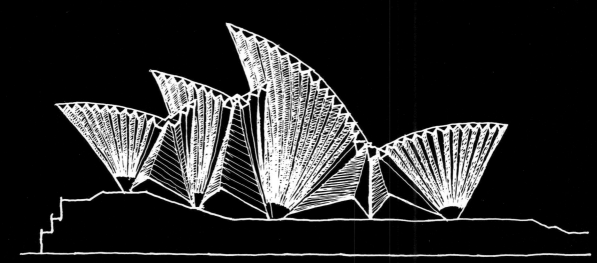

Spherical scheme, Jan 1962 (L): small circle ridge, great circle rib profile, insitu & precast r.c.

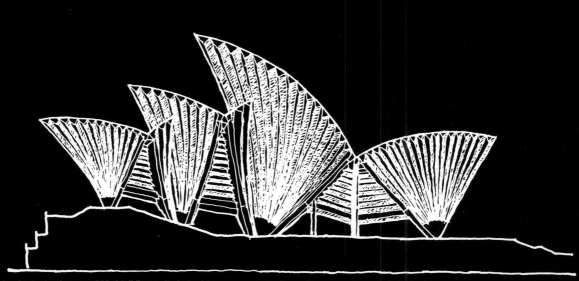

Final spherical scheme, 1962–63 (M): small circle ridge, great circle rib profile, precast r.c. partially insitu.

SEPT 18	Sunday: Ashworth dep. London 1200 hrs.
SEPT 21	Wednesday: Ashworth arr. Sydney 1320 hrs. and later reports on progress to the Sydney Opera House Executive Committee (SOHEC).
SEPT 30	Elvira, Spain, competition announced for a new Mediterranean town.
OCT 19	Balslev & Partners, Copenhagen, ask to withdraw as electrical engineering consultants for the project.
OCT	Bar area re–design for Major & Minor Halls' widening of seating area in the auditoria to compensate for loss of seats resulting from the abolition of the separate balcony. The corridor solution was designed by Mikami based on his idea of leg–and–knee joint.
OCT 29	Discussion of bar area between Utzon, Kelman and Mikami.
OCT 29	Resignation of James Thomas, Charles Hall (U.S.A.), Odd Lovset from the Hellebæk office.
OCT 31	Meeting held at Hellebæk office to finalise the matter of Balslev & Partners (the electrical consultants) between Arup, Jenkins and Utzon (Oct 31 to Dec 3).
NOV 1	Ronald Jenkins arrives and joins discussion.
NOV 4	Skipper Nielsen leaves Denmark for Sydney.
NOV 9	Wednesday: Paul Robeson gives a concert to more than 250 workmen at Bennelong Point and is mobbed afterwards.
NOV 14	Monday: Utzon dep. Copenhagen to Sydney for meetings starting 1 Dec., 1960, on Waagner–Biro Stage machinery, brings Stroh, Sedlaczek & Weiss. R. Kelman visits Hellebæk office till 18th.
NOV 16	N. Mollmann joins discussion on shell rib system, louvre plane etc.
NOV 22	Utzon leaves for Sydney on Tuesday evening.
NOV 24	Mikami travels to Berlin with Jens Arup (Ove Arup's son) to attend 'Berlin Colloquium uber Theaterbau'.
NOV 24	Jenkins writes that Utzon has 'kept himself free of engagements to concentrate on guiding architectural development personally'. Arup, Jenkins, Mollman and Kelman from the Arup office make frequent visits to Hellebæk office.

Fredensborg housing 1962–63

DEC 1   Farewell party for Osmond & Valerie Jarvis who return to Sydney.

DEC 6   First pair of concourse beams J6 & J7 are poured and prove highly unsatisfactory; walls
             thickened from 7 to 9 inches between sections 6 & 7.

DEC 20   Utzon returns from Sydney visit.

DEC 22   Christmas holidays break ends 8 January 1961.

1961

JAN 1   **Ralph Symonds** drowns while rock fishing at Barrenjoey Head.

JAN 11   Discussion: Mikami with H. Mollmann on Restaurant shells. In Sydney: J4 & J5 concourse beams are
             poured over 12 hours; mixing plant breaks down.

JAN 12   Four engineers from Waagner–Biro visit Hellebæk office. Final check of Major Hall Bar area drawings.

JAN 13   Prof. Unruh, Waagner–Biro engineers, discuss stage machinery.

JAN 27	Discussion with Utzon about balconies, stage towers, south foyer etc.; R. Jenkins writes to J. Utzon, *'we went to all this trouble because of the shells being structurally the wrong shape as we pointed out to you right from the beginning.'*
FEB 9	Discussion between Utzon & Mikami on shell cantilever, louvre plane etc.
FEB 14	Date of Yuzo Mikami's wedding is fixed for 3rd March at Munich.
FEB 20	Land purchase by Jørn Utzon at Bayview of Lot. 1, D.P. 27991 created by transfer No. H 127938. Area: 4a. 3r. 10p; gives his address as Hellebæk, Denmark; takes out mortgage with Alfred Conrad Blumet, Robert George Blumet & Alfred John Blumet on 14 April 1961. Discharged debt 16 August 1962.
FEB 28	Last day for Yuzo Mikami at Hellebæk office.
MAR 1	Mikami leaves Denmark for Munich; he has three jobs for Japanese airline offices and asks Mogens Prip–Buus to assist him for the year prior to starting working with Ove Arup in London.
MAR 14	*Opera House Trust, Act No. 9* is assented to setting up an interim body corporate under the name of the Sydney Opera House Trust (SOHT) which is to ensure the proper planning and organisation necessary in respect of the completion and subsequent functioning of the Opera house, to hold office from the passing of the measure until 2 years after completion of the building. The intention of the bill was to transfer the members of the existing opera house executive committee (SOHEC) to the first trust (SOHT). The Act states that the Trust has four functions:
	A — the administration, care, control, management and maintenance of the Opera House and its site;
	B — the management and administration of the Opera House as a theatre, concert hall, and place of assembly for the presentation of any of the branches of the musical, operatic, dancing, visual or auditory arts or as a meeting place in respect of matters of international, national or local significance;
	C — the promotion of artistic taste and achievement in any of the arts just referred to;
	D — and Scientific research into and the encouragement of new and improved forms of presentation and methods of entertainment.
	The Minister for Works is nominated President of the Trust, the Lord Mayor as Vice–President, and Mr Haviland, Chairman. This made him Chairman of the Executive Committee (SOHEC) and the Trust (SOHT) at the same time. The Trust to consist of 15 members, some of whom are members of the SOHEC or sit on its advisory panels.
APR	Introduction of circular arc rib roof scheme with surface generated by circular arcs spanning between pedestal and ridge parabola.
APR 12	Wednesday 2.30 p.m.: First meeting of Sydney Opera House Trust (SOHT) comprising 17 members in

the office of Premier of NSW. The other 15 members were to be the current 15 members of the SOHEC. Thus, the membership of the SOHEC was the same as the SOHT, excluding the Premier and the Lord Mayor, with Mr. Haviland as Chairman. 2nd meeting of SOHT on 9 May, coincided with 41th of SOHEC.

JUNE **Ronald Jenkins** (OA & P), then an associate partner (died early 1980s), withdraws from SOH project out of frustration, and **Hugo H. Mollman**, the associate directly responsible for the job, leaves Ove Arup in protest. Both were strongly committed to parabolic geometry in schemes B through F (June 1961). **Jack Zunz** takes charge of the roof design team in London and supervises tail end of Stage I.

Ellipsoid scheme introduced for roof with surface generated by circular arcs spanning between pedestal springing and parabolic ridge section. Superseded by Scheme H — ellipsoidal scheme having elliptical ridge profile and elliptical rib profile, insitu and precast reinforced concrete.

Ove Arup goes to Denmark with a roof scheme of one shell that had folds underneath. When he comes back Zunz and 2 senior people work out the possibilities. Propose scheme 1: a steel structure with a concrete skin on the outside and inside; shells no longer interconnected (G). By autumn 1961 there is a radical change of design of the roof vaults remarked upon by Arup.

> **ZUNZ**
>
> Gerhard Jacob Zunz, b. Moenchengladbach, Germany, 25 December 1926–, s. Wilhelm and Helene (Isenbach) Z, m. Babs Maisel, 1948. B Sc in Civil Engineering from U. Witwerstrand, Johannesburg, SA, 1948, 1948–50, co–founding partner of OA & P South Africa, 1954–1959.

Jørn Utzon writes to editor of *Arckitekten* 'Om Stockholm–universitet', Sep. 1961, p. 290, criticising Henning Larsen for using his idea of plateaus and pointing out similarity of Stockholm University scheme with his earlier Competition scheme for World Exhibition, Copenhagen, 1959, in *Zodiac no. 10*, p. 124–125.

AUG 16 Jørn Utzon discharges mortgage for land purchase at Bayview in April 14.

AUTUMN Utzon's Hellebæk villa office now overcrowded with a staff numbering upwards of 20 people — some new architects engaged while Utzon was visiting Sydney. Office is relocated in a better house at Kildekrog approximately 10 kilometres south of Hellebæk.

AUG 29 Utzon booked at Athenaeum Court Hotel, Piccadilly, from 29 Aug. to 1 September, to discuss two rival shell schemes, chooses the ribbed vault alternative in OA & P's office in presence of Zunz.

SEPT 1 **Eero Saarinen** dies at Ann Arbor, Michigan, aged 51.

SEPT   The G & H schemes offered to Utzon. A meeting is held in Ove Arup's office with Jack Zunz and Jørn Utzon present. Utzon replies: 'I don't care what it costs, I don't care what scandal it causes, I don't care how long it takes, but that's what I want.' He chose the ribbed ellipsoidal Scheme J with ribbed profile — not G or H.

Zunz looks at ways to put Scheme J together.

Spherical scheme introduced with triangular ribbed soffit, ridge elevation part of a small circle and radial ribs a circular arc from a great circle of constant radius. Development proceeds to December 1962 before Utzon's departure to Australia.

SEPT 20   Rider & Hunt estimate the cost for Stage I to III: £9,300,000.

OCT   **Kev Nagle** rings Zunz to say Utzon has solved roof by making the shells spherical; results in Scheme K, small circle profile, great circle rib profile., insitu & precast RC.

Aage Hartvig Petersen drawn–plans of Opera House now completed showing radial shell over Minor Hall and facetted triangular shell over the Major Hall.

Major Hall, scheme II, with the orchestra in the middle carried out in detail by Utzon's office. Models made at 1 : 10 scale with a variety of seating types and orchestra arrangements; Gabler and Cremer study the scheme, feel it is feasible.

OCT 6   Opera House Executive Committee accepts recommendation for the nominated contractor for Stage II.

OCT 20   Ove Arup writes to Ashworth describing the critical breakthrough to a spherical geometry for the roof shells.

OCT 30   Minister appoints the nominated contractor Hornibrooks for stage II.

NOV 21   Tuesday: Utzon visits Ove Arup Office in London; Hornibrooks due there on 28 November a week later.

DEC   Henning Larsen scheme for University of Stockholm published in *Arkitekten*, no. 12, 1961, pp. 217–227.

DEC 4   Ashworth informed of the new roof shape.

1962

 1962–63   Danish Co–operative Building Company Housing Development, Fredensborg, Denmark. Fredensborg is located 50 km north of Copenhagen. The success of the Kingo Houses, inspired Dansk Samvirke, through lawyer Valdemar Hvidt, to propose a project for a small development consisting of single–family houses for members of their society. Danske Samvirke Foreningen, Copenhagen, is a support organisation for Danish citizens who spend long periods abroad on business as technical advisors in the Foreign Service.

JAN   Yuzo Mikami joins OA & P as personal assistant to Ove Arup and works with him on the Kingsgate Footbridge at Durham (1964).

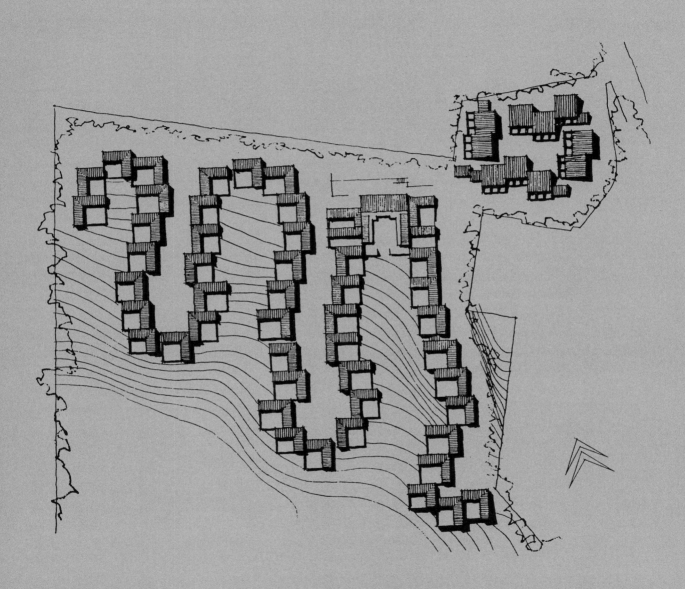

Fredensborg, Denmark, plan.

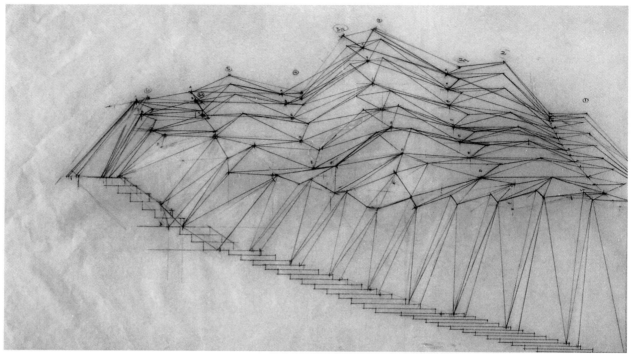

Major Hall longitudinal section, Nov. 21, 1962 (ML. PXD 492, f. 434)

Spherical roof geometry drawing rib plan of Minor Hall with 16 ribs, Nov. 1962. (ML. PXD 492 ff. 385)

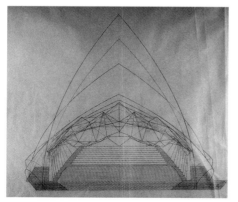

Major Hall cross section 22nd Nov. (ML. PXD 492)

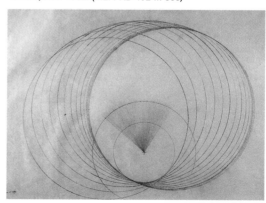

Business Cards are FREE at www.vistaprint.com!

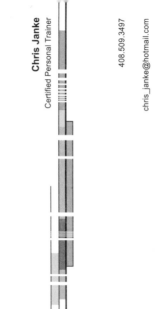

Chris Janke

Certified Personal Trainer

408.509.3497

chris_janke@hotmail.com

■■ **JAN**	***Yellow Book*** submitted, includes further plans by Utzon and notes by his consultants. During 1960 Utzon developed an idea of abolishing the separate balcony and replacing it with a cantilevered balcony to extend the main seating area. The Yellow book drawings show two slightly different forms. Seating capacity: 2,700 concerts, 1,722 opera; volume: 960,000 c.ft. concert, 680,000 c.ft. opera; dimensions: width 126ft, length (opera) 107ft. Minor Hall was drawn by **Jon Lundberg** (later became Head of Oslo School of Architecture), the Major Hall drawn by **Oktay Nayman** (see p. 28. *Yellow book*) was not ready in time for Utzon's planned 1 March departure from New York.
JAN 8–19	Ove Arup is ill, has fainting attacks, recurs Jan. 22–25. Spends Feb. 1–12 at Bad Gadstein, Austria, for treatment, and from March 8 till April 9, he rests at home.
FEB 13	Successful Höganäs tile tender £2.2.6 per sq yd, well under other Australian quotations, vindicates Utzon's methods.
MAR 1	Thurs. 10.07 a.m. American Airlines Boeing 707 jet carrying 87 passengers and 8 crew members takes off from New York International Airport at Idlewild bound for Los Angeles, climbs to 800 ft (244m), suddenly nose dives into Jamaica Bay killing everyone on board. Ove Arup's drawings were late so trip to Australia advanced by one fortnight to 14 March. Utzon and Jack Zunz planned to meet in New York, from where they were booked on an American Airlines Flight One to Los Angeles.
MARCH 14	Wednesday: Utzon and Jack Zunz fly into Sydney, arr. 7.15 a.m. to testify to the SOH/Technical Advisory Panel, break the news of the change in the roof. After a brief site inspection in the morning Utzon and Zunz retire in early afternoon to a hotel at Bondi and sleep — not to be disturbed till 11 a.m. on Wednesday 25th March. Utzon with his strong visual and verbal presentation, carries all before him
MAR 15	Thursday: site inspection of class–C formwork. Only a small number of folded slabs poured; at 2.30 p.m. meeting held with the site staff to discuss distortion of forms and unsatisfactory finish.
MAR 16	Friday: meeting with Tech Advisory Panel; Utzon & Zunz present the schemes for Stages II & III.
MAR 17 & 18	Saturday. & Sunday: meeting with contractor.
MAR 19	Monday: meeting with contractor.
MAR 20	Tuesday: SOHEC Meeting: Utzon & Zunz table Stage II. Afternoon meeting with Minister PWD and Deputy Director PWD. Minister outlines the political position and requests information on total costs, completion date, stage lighting, situation with regard to other contractors for Stage II.
MAR 21	Wednesday: meeting with Hornibrook at Ashfield; model of erection of ribs.
MAR 22	Thursday: meeting of Tech. Advisory Panel, report on negotiations with Hornibrook.
MAR 23	Friday: meeting with quantity surveyor on estimates, site inspection.

MAR 25	Sunday: discussions on site with Zunz on structural quality of the job.
MAR 26	Monday: meeting with site office, Utzon & Zunz consider off–form concrete problems; meet Dusseldorp on Civil & & Civic's claim.
MAR 27	Tuesday: meet with Tech Advisory Panel — design of mechanical services.
MAR 28	Wednesday: final discussion of estimate; visit to Ralph Symonds factory in afternoon to inspect wall panels, toilet cubicles, cloak rooms.
MAR 29	Thursday: Technical Advisory Panel, estimate tabled; Utzon presents recommendation on tiling tender; meets Dusseldorp in the afternoon.
MAR 30	Friday: meeting with Tech Advisory Panel; explanation of development of parking schemes for SOH; new system for external cladding with precast panels.
MAR 31	Saturday: Utzon & Zunz meet Dusseldorp on site; Utzon explains importance of precision of formwork for folded slab.
APR 2	Monday: meeting with Dusseldorp negotiations continue on extra claims.
APR 3	Tuesday: Tech Advis Panel meeting on the stage machinery and estimate.
APR 4	Wednesday: site visit by Lord Mayor of Sydney, Melbourne and Brisbane, Sir Malcolm Sargent.
APR 5	Thursday: meetings with Pilkington Bros, Austral Bronze, Mr Yates (PWD); yet another meeting with Mr Dusseldorp; meeting with Mr Humphrey, Ass. Dir. PWD.
APR 6	Friday: Meet of SOHEC; time of completion adopted recommendations of Stage II; estimate adopted; Utzon outlines proposal for precast concrete panels; Premier visits the site later that morning.
APR 9	Monday: Visit to Ralph Symonds Homebush factory to see completed mock–ups of toilet cubicle; discuss timing schedule and scope of work.
APR 10	Tuesday: meeting of Tech Advis Panel — Utzon reports on Premier's visit, approval of all reports; notes estimate might not go to Cabinet. Hornibrook's engineer's leave for London. Visit ends Utzon & Zunz depart Sydney 10 April.
APR	Rider & Hunt estimate the cost of SOH: £13,750,000 ($27.5M).
APR 2	Mr Sørensen of Zeuthen & Sørensen visit Sydney speak to Stanley Darling at ABC.
MAY 24	FN Meet. #29: following meeting with OA & P in London, the inside and outside details of the shells nearly completed.
MAY 29	**Ian Mackenzie** (OA & P Sydney) telephones Zunz, London, requesting termination of Civil & Civic.
JUNE 1	Dept Copenhagen for Berlin, visits Staatsoper with Unruh, Ulmer, Gabler and Prof Cremer; introduced to acoustics of Berlin Opera House.

JUNE 2	Utzon with Gabler visit Berlin Philharmonic Hall; meeting at Hotel Hilton — Utzon explains drawings of SOH. It is decided Mr Gabler and Prof Cremer should do model tests for acoustics of Major and Minor Halls as second opinion but without replacing Dr Jordan. Utzon and Lundberg attend Berliner Staatsoper performance of Arnold Schoenberg's 'Moses und Aron'.
JUNE 3	Utzon leaves Berlin for Vienna.
JUNE 4	Meeting at Waagner–Biro office: new drawings of the stage tower presented for both halls, Bob Kelman from London gives results from OA & P.
JUNE 5	Morning meeting with W–B., afternoon visit to Theatre Sur Stadt, Vienna, special performance of 'Don Carlos'.
JUNE 6	Meetings all day at W–B to discuss details of both stage towers. In the evening observes scenery changes at the Wiener Staatsoper during performance of Wagner's 'Gotterdammerung'.
JUNE 7	Morning, meeting W–B, detailed discussions.
JUNE 8	Lundberg, Weiss, Hillinger visit Burgteater, Vienna, witness setting up of scenery for next performance. Depart for Salzburg in the afternoon.
JUNE 9	Visit to Salzburg Festspielhaus; afternoon dept Salzburg for Vienna.
JUNE 10	Depts. Vienna and returns to Copenhagen.
JULY 2	Jørn Utzon and family away on holidays for 3 weeks until 22 July.
JULY 3	Jørn Utzon answers his critics in interview in Copenhagen, *SMH*, 38,885, July 3, p. 2.
AUG 21	SOHEC meet #54, decides (Aug 21, 1962, p. 5): *'The Government considered it should not rely on the advice of one firm of consultants but another Consultant should, in collaboration with the existing Consultants, examine the data available…the Government required a second opinion and there was no alternative but for the Committee to comply.'*
AUG 22	Cabinet approves proposed contract with M.R. Hornibrook (NSW) Pty Ltd in respect of Stage II.
AUG 23	Cabinet sub–committee comprising Heffron (Premier), Ryan (Minister for PWD) and Pat Hills, representing NSW government, convene a meeting with Ove Arup, Jørn Utzon and Jack Zunz, the purpose of which is to reassure the client. Ove Arup is unwell at the time — but despite being out of action for some months, he travels to Australia. Ove Arup commented at the time: *'the whole project is in jeopardy.'* On the flight to Australia, the Ove Arup team met Utzon at Hawaii and have dinner together and agree that Zunz and Utzon should do all the talking; instead, in Sydney, Ove Arup takes over meeting and talks for 45 minutes non–stop. A few minor exchanges after this and meeting ends. All the government required was a second opinion.
	The same day, Utzon, Arup & Zunz have a 5 hour conference with the Opera House Executive Committee to discuss costs and their escalation in response to pressure from the Liberal–Country Party Opposition.

Yves Guion (French), known for prestressing work in concrete, spends one week with project and writes letter to NSW government confirming all the principles on which the design is based.

AUG 24   Press statement issued giving up–to–date estimate of £12,500,000 cost to complete the SOH project.

Mr Minoru Takeyama (b. Sapporo 1934–) comes to Denmark and joins design team at Hellebæk; he works on the foyer and the glass walls of SOH. He describes how Utzon: *'…to get the design for the shell he would get wooden balls shaped like a Danish cheese and put them in a bathtub. Then by studying the angles at which the water cut the surface he was able to come up with the correct geometrical pattern.'*

AUG   **Menzies government deploys to South Vietnam 30 instructors as the Australian Army Training Team Vietnam.**

AUG 30   Prof Cremer praises Utzon's latest arrangement with 'Weinbergstufen' (vineyard terraces) for concert hall.

SEPT 4   Jørn Utzon is issued with passport Nr. 1114830 at Helsingør, expires, Dep. 4, 1967. Height stated as 194 cm (6ft 4.3 in), blond hair, blue eyes.

SEPT 6   Weekly Meet #31, Hellebæk: architect's newest layout for restaurant area.

OCT   Ashworth calls on Utzon in Denmark and meets Prof Unruh for discussion of contract for the stage lighting re Siemens's offer.

Major Hall: crystalline radial ceiling scheme finalised to resemble a cavern.

OCT 15   beginnings of vineyard terrace system of seating in the Major Hall at back of stage area.

OCT 18   contract for the new precast–element rib roof system is let by the NSW Dep of Public Works to M.R. Hornibrook (N.S.W.) P/L.

NOV 11   Major Hall ceiling supported by radial ribs, radial geometry now resembles Minor Hall.

NOV 14   P. Beckman (OA & P) visits Utzon at Hellebæk Office and establishes the structural design principles for the windows and auditorium ceilings between Nov. 14 to 16, 1962, in report dated 19 Nov. ML MSS 2362, item 32, #455–467 (231162).

NOV 21   Jørn Utzon purchases land at Bayview (Lot 62, D.P. 30648: area 1a. Or. 0p).

NOV 20   SOHEC Meet. #57: PWD Director writes to Chairman Haviland stating that PWD is Constructing Authority responsible for the project; the Committee is responsible to the Minister; expresses concern over the substantial increase in the estimate of cost; and insists the estimated cost is £12.5 million ($25M) must be adhered to.

NOV 25   Meeting at Hellebæk with Arup, Zunz, Lewis: Minor Hall to have structural system using concave laminated timber beams of constant radius but varying length. Weight of Auditorium cladding given as 100 kg/m^2.

NOV 27		Prof Cremer, Berlin submits his Report: *3 stellungnahme zur raumakustischen Gestaltung der major und minor hall des Sydney Opera House.*
DEC 26		Boxing Day, Monday: Utzon and family leave Copenhagen on journey to Australia, booked in overnight at Heathrow A.P. London. Closed his office at Hellebæk. Zunz hires room at circular shaped The Aerial Hotel, Heathrow Airport, and meeting starts at 3.20 p.m., goes till 11 p.m. in evening with break for dinner. Ove Arup, Jack Zunz, Michael Lewis, Yuzo Mikami, Joe Huan and Jørn Utzon are present. Snow and freezing weather outside. Discussion ranged across pending problems in the design of the roof shells and the tile lids, their spacing and clarification of many details of the shells and tile lids, as well as fixing the final outline of the shell geometry prior to Utzon's departure. Meeting ended on the friendliest of terms. Utzon was not able to be contacted until March 4, 1963. At this time, OA & P have employed a team of 50 to 60 people on the SOH project.

1963

	Utzon, Lis and children fly to U.S.A. and travel for 4–5 weeks examining ideas for SOH. Later, Jack Zunz claimed Utzon was incommunicado for the duration of the trip, but from his sickbed with the flu at the Windjammer Inn, Miami, Utzon wrote to Zunz about the job on 21 Jan.
JAN	Stage I completed for $5,160,000.
FEB	Utzon's new office is established on Bennelong Point work site.
FEB 19	Last two west concourse beams poured.
FEB 20	Sydney Opera House (Amendment) Bill debated in Legislative Assembly (see *Hansard* No. 38, Parliamentary Debates, 40th Parliament–2nd Session, pp. 2649–2653).
LATE FEB	Utzon and family holiday one week on Tahiti.
MAR 1	Friday: Ove Arup and several of his partners due in Sydney.
MAR 3	Sunday: **Queen Elizabeth II** and the **Duke of Edinburgh** slip away from Government House after luncheon and spend almost half–an–hour climbing over the half–completed podium structure on windy Bennelong Point.
MAR 4	Monday: Utzon family fly to Sydney on March 4, aboard early morning flt T.A. 1 from Tahiti, arriving around 11.00 a.m. In transit, Utzon received an invitation to lunch on the Royal Yacht Britannia the same day by radio. They are greeted at airport by **Mr R.M. Thompson** (secretary of the opera House Executive Committee) and **Mr S.N. Nicklin** (Macdonald Wagner and Priddle the consulting engineers).
	Lis and Jørn Utzon have lunch with the royal party on board Britannia at 1 p.m. several hours after arriving in Sydney; meet **Patrick White** and Utzon later shows White around SOH Stage I.

MAR 5   In an interview, Utzon reveals he plans to stay in Australia till SOH is completed in 1965 and he plans to build home at Bayview on land purchased the previous year (March 1962). During his stay in Sydney, Utzon rented the following residences: 19 Alexandra crescent Bayview (March 1964–Sep 65); cnr. Ebor & Cynthea Roads, PALM BEACH (Sep 1965– April 14, 1966).

His main office was at Opera House Site Office, Bennelong Point, Sydney, opposite entrance to the Royal Botanic Gardens on extreme eastern corner of site.

In Oct 1964, Utzon opened a second office at Goddard's Boat shed at 118 Iluka Road on Snapperman Beach at the corner of Iluka and Barrenjoey Road.

Kim Utzon was enrolled at Loquat Valley School (Anglican Preparatory School) 197 Pittwater Rd, Bayview. After they moved to Palm Beach, Kim moved to Avalon Public School. Lin Utzon attended Narrabeen High School, on Namona & Pittwater Rd, Narrabeen till 1964, and later enrolled in Art at East Sydney Tech.

MAR 6   Wed. Second reading debate on *SOH (amendment) Bill* (Parliamentary debates 40th Parliament–2nd Session, *Hansard* No. 44, pp. 3095–3143).

MAR 7   Thursday: Second reading speech by Mr N. Ryan on *The Sydney Opera House Amendment Bill* with cost set at £12.5 M (A$25 M).

MAR 10   Sunday: interview in *Sun Herald* in which Utzon describes his vision for the Bayview house.

Civil & Civic vacate Bennelong Point worksite.

MAR 15   Utzon shows Patrick White and Manoly Lascaris over the Opera House. White comments later: *'It has made me feel glad I am alive in Australia today. At last we are going to have something worth having.'*

MAR 17   *'Blunder revealed'*, demolition of 20 reinforced concrete column supports in base. *Sunday Mirror*, p. 1.

MAR 25   Hornibrook take possession of site, commence work on Stage 2.

MAR 26   Ove Arup writes to the Minister for Works to vary the arrangement and free OA & P from responsibility for consulting work except Structural and civil engineering. The Government agrees to this, henceforth, other consultants to work directly with Utzon and be paid on his say–so.

APR   Rider Hunt estimate of SOH cost: £13,993,000 (A$27,986,000).

APR 5   **Michael Lewis** arrives in Sydney on crutches after a bus accident at Tel Aviv.

APR 20   Professor Unruh visits Sydney.

MAY 1   Demolition of shell columns by G. Bayutti P/L, starts in morning and takes four months at cost of £A17,600 ($35,200).

MAY 5   **Frank D'Arcy** joins B.P. office, works on glass walls, resigns 30 October 1964 because of lack of work — everything halted after Utzon moved to Goddard's Boat Shed at Palm Beach.

MAY 12   **Bill Wheatland,** formerly university architect at Monash University, joins Utzon in May, soon after Frank D'Arcy; refuses to do further tile lid pattern drawings with Frank D'Arcy; Utzon confronts him and he promises he is his man, but does no more drawing work and is appointed an administrator, attends meetings.

MAY 21   First sketches of the Bayview House at Kara Crescent.

Art Museum, Silkeborg, Jutland (project), scheme for an underground museum, drawing done in one week by Oktay Nayman.

Zunz comments: *'so there were a few clouds appearing then in early 1963, in our relationship, which I don't think, after that, ever really — once he was in Australia, it really went downhill.'* In 1963, OA & P established a 'building group' led by Philip Dowson, the founding architectural partner.

JUNE   An excited Utzon writes to historian S. Giedion telling him of his spatial geometry solution to the Sydney Opera House employing only movable formwork based on segments in shape of a sphere, arrived at between May and October 1961 in Utzon's office at Hellebæk.

JUNE 25   Utzon to Cremer: *'Sir Bernard Heinze will be visiting a number of countries in Europe…'*. Heinz was Director of the NSW Conservatorium of Music until his retirement in 1966. The Berlin Philharmonic Hall (1956–63) was completed on Oct.15, 1963. Insecure and unimpressive as a conductor, Heinz was more exceptional as an organiser and publicist.

JUNE 27   Utzon submits his design for the exhibition pavilion to SOHEC and estimate of A£3,500 for approval. A different design was erected by PWD day labour on the Tarpeian Way landing.

JUNE 30   <u>Total fees paid to Utzon in 1962–63 financial year: A£87,361.0.5.</u>

JULY   Zürich Theatre Competition conditions issued (organised by Bauamt II der Stadt Zurich, with Prize of 100,000 Fr), is accompanied by an essay by the Swiss writer and playwright **Max Frisch** who was an excellent architect before he switched to writing. Competition was open to all Swiss architects plus five invited foreigners:Bourbonnais, van den Broek & Bakema, Scharoun, Siren, Utzon. 97 schemes were entered.

JULY 17   Meeting at Utzon's site office stresses the importance of accurate concrete work.

AUG 14   Utzon writes to Chairman SOHEC/TAP, warning of a possible 12–month delay if Hornibrook is not made head contractor for Stage III.

AUG 20   SOHEC Meet #66: demolition of shell columns by G. Bayutti–Contractors P/L starting May 1. Complaints arose following press publicity. Ashworth report from TAP (Technical Advisory Panel) to follow Utzon's recommendation that he be authorised to negotiate with M.R. Hornibrook (NSW) Pty Ltd to undertake head contract for Stage III. Sir William Holford praises Utzon's exposition of SOH.

AUG 24   Werner Gabler writes to Utzon, Sydney, six days later on Aug 30, that Sir Bernard Heinze has visited Berlin where he sought to clarify the one question: *'the viability of having a seating arrangement in the Major Hall whereby part of the audience is sitting behind the orchestra. Sir Bernard Heinze belongs to a class of conductors who basically does not wish to see any audience behind the musicians. I was unable to convince him that it would [be] irresponsible as an alternative to move the orchestra further towards the back of the stage tower,…It just so happened that the new hall in the Philharmony here in Berlin has progressed so far in construction, that its final form and the arrangement of the seating on all sides of the orchestral podium are recognisable…'*

AUG 30   Cremer to Utzon: comments on Utzon's arrangement of 'Weinberg stufen' which ameliorated former solution but was not optimal. Suggests use of plywood sandwich panel construction consisting of thin panel 8kg/m², 8cm air space filled with fibreglass, plus thicker panel of 20 kg/m² gypsum sheets 2 cm and or plywood 3 cm.

Utzon files for patent AN IMPROVED ROOFING CONSTRUCTION AND BUILDING ELEMENTS THEREOF, Application No. 34,837/63, Commonwealth Patent Specification No. 271062 for a system of plywood U–Beams Utzon planned to use them on the roof of the Bayview House. Application Lodged 10 Aug, 1964; accepted 31 Oct, 1966; published 10 Feb, 1966; application prepared by M. Starfield Patent Attorney.

SEPT   Rider Hunt cost estimate of SOH: £A14,799,529 ($29,599,058).

SEPT 4   Newspaper articles say state government powerless to control costs.

SEPT 13   Schauspielhaus Competition, Zurich: closing date for competitor's questions.

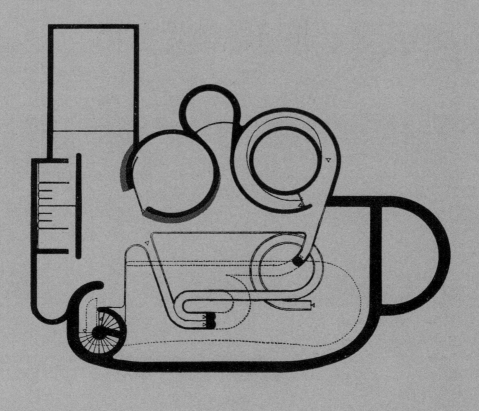

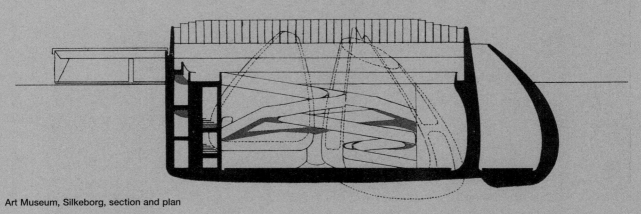

Art Museum, Silkeborg, section and plan

SEPT 18 Meeting with PWD at Utzon's site off: R.A.P. Johnson, C. Humphrey, Walker, Utzon, Maclurcan to discuss what constitutes Stage III. Utzon interrogated by Johnson who considers *'that the Technical Advisory Panel [TAP] should be used extensively for advice on the architectural side of Stage III, and should approve any decision for the P.W.D. with the Minister's right of veto. He did not think that the Minister, having appointed such an august body, would contradict their decisions.'*

SEPT Major Hall: crystalline triangular faceted auditorium ceiling is abandoned in favour of a new convex scheme inspired by Minor Hall. Both Cremer and Gabler still support the ceiling acoustically, but there are problems with the seating arrangement under it.

SEPT 10 Utzon and Lundberg attempt to deal with problems that Cremer highlighted on their return to Sydney in *SOH 947*–Revised Seating Arrangement, the seating behind orchestra is reduced and side seats lifted in a vineyard arrangement.

OCT 10 Utzon writes to Helge Hjertholm: *'the situation here is very positive and stimulating now and have glass wall and Minor Hall under control and Major Hall with 2,800 seats in front of the orchestra.'*

OCT 14 Tenders for the stage towers steelwork received by OA & P.

OCT 15 Berlin Philharmonic hall designed by Hans Scharoun is opened with concert conducted by Herbert von Karajan performing Beethoven's *9th Symphony.*

OHEC meet: Utzon states that Concert Hall is to have audience on one (north) side of the orchestra. A£40,000 is allocated for mock–ups. Ralph Symonds builds a roof of 55 ft (16.8m) plywood elements pre–fabricated in its factory. Rear stage walls complete.

OCT 21 Drawing *SOH 972*: Major Hall Revised Seating Arrangement with the audience in front (north) of orchestra. This entails a new ceiling profile. Cremer and Gabler reject the scheme on Nov 2.

NOV 6 Music Panel endorses Utzon's revised scheme. The new scheme is a variant of the original scheme with a long hall and 3,000 seats in front of the orchestra. Designed as multiple–use hall with concerts set as number one priority.

NOV 11 Lundberg to Cremer: *'I Would like to point out that these new drawings…We are aware that these changes of the Major Hall seating are followed by changes of volume of the space and the necessity of another ceiling profile, and that this may throw all the work done up till now in the waste–paper basket, but so many factors were against the other solution…'.*

NOV 14 Lundberg makes *SOH 1039*: Major Hall — Plan of Hall and Longitudinal Section, with different positions for orchestra. It shows new seating arrangement.

NOV 18 Tec. Advis. Panel. approves new Main Hall proposal which Utzon claims can seat 2,850.

Berlin Philharmonic by Hans Scharaun. The vineyard terraces of the auditorium were adopted for the Sydney Opera House Major Hall.

NOV 19 Pedestal 5.1 cast in preparation for placement of pre–cast concrete ribs.

NOV 21 First pre–cast unit for roof scheduled to be placed in position.

NOV 21 Utzon purchases land at Bayview from William Peter Gaha of St.Ives for £4,145 ($8,290); gives his address as No. 19 Alexandra Crescent, Bayview. The land is Lot 62, D.P. 30648 (Vol. 9237, fol.138).

NOV 22 Lundberg completes drawing *SOH 1040* showing Major Hall internal contours of shells related to radial axes of hall and confuses the 2.44m (8ft) clearance line for services with the actual shell soffit profile — his crucial mistake is not discovered until Jan 10, 1966.

DEC 2 Lunberg makes *SOH 1045* Reverberation Time Limit Curves for Main Hall and this defines the position of steps in the ceiling.

DEC 6 Interviewed in Copenhagen, Ove Arup comments, *'I'm playing around with problems... I am slowly retiring'*.

DEC The Dec. 1963 completion date, set for SOH in 1960, is passed.

1963–64 Utzon buys a 30ft, 1 ton, plywood construction Yachting World Keel Boat, Diamond Class, 1st built by Hans Erickson, at Newport, and named it 'Kim.' It had a black diamond on its sail and was designed by Jack Holt of England. He sailed on Wednesday afternoons with Fred Edgington a member of Royal Prince Alfred Yachting Club.

1964

The Building Group of OA & P becomes Arup Associates and Australian Partnership formed. Ashworth (Ass. 1949, Fellow 1950, RAIA) moves from University of Sydney and is appointed Dean of the Faculty of Architecture at University of NSW.

New Main Hall program is agreed in early 1964 when Utzon switched over from an audience on two–sides to audience on one–side of the orchestra. Entirely new problems arose because of this change. After some months, a new 'Roman' theatre with three balconies was abandoned mainly for acoustic reasons and four alternatives were developed in its place.

FEB 17 Utzon explains his glass wall scheme to Ralph Symonds Ltd and OA & P and says that the scheme is a development of his patented plywood roof element system from 1963.

FEB 20 Ralph Symonds Ltd announces a trading loss of A£200,000 for the half year ended 31 December 1963, in addition to stocks written down by about A£170,000.

FEB 26 Receivers appointed to Ralph Symonds Ltd.

FEB 28 Schauspielhaus Competition, Zurich, closing date for submission of entries.

MAR 5	**William Walter Wood** F.R.I.B.A., M.I. Struct. E., a departmental architect in the supervision branch, is appointed by Director to act as liaison architect between Utzon office and PWD.
MAR 13	Schauspielhaus Zurich: submission of model.
MAR 23	Utzon holds discussions with Haviland, Ashworth, Parkes, Thomson concerning Mr Wood and insists that he be denied access to documents. Ashworth points out that there were no technical people in charge of PWD. Utzon prophesied that the PWD's influence could prove disastrous in the future.
MAR 31	Estimate of plywood in SOH by Mr Ezra: Major Hall 27,100 ft² and Minor Hall 19,000 ft² of 4 inch laminate elements.
APR 1	Rider Hunt estimate of SOH cost: A£17,200,000 ($34,400,000).
APR 8	Analysis of plywood costs, Major Hall A£142,932 ($285,864), Minor Hall A£93,360 ($186,720).
APR 10	Mr. Nutsch visits Utzon in Sydney until May 19; compiles documentation on behalf of Prof. Cremer to assist in the acoustic, Prof Walther Unruh from Berlin visits Sydney in April.
APR 17	**Leif Oberg Utzon**, Jørn's elder brother dies suddenly in Paris aged 48 years of a heart attack. He was a chemical engineer and his death came as a great shock to Utzon who became concerned over his own health. Utzon left for Europe before this and returned sometime after his brother's funeral.
	R. Maclurcan writes to Utzon on figures given to Minister and his response. Utzon writes to Maclurcan from Hellebæk saying, *'But the situation in my family is not too good but there is hope now.'*
APR 20	Utzon announces plans to erect Major Hall glass wall at beginning of April 1965.
APR 24	Meeting at Utzon's office: Lundberg tables general layout for Minor Hall Auditorium *SOH 948* which shows internal and external skin 3'o" apart with external surfaces 8'o" below soffit of shells.

WOOD

Bill Wood was registered in NSW, 27 September 1961 cert. No. 2080. Wood originally came from South Africa where he had an architectural practice; academically well qualified, in 1962 Wood was a supervising architect in NSW Dep. of Pub. Works responsible for Goldstein Hall, UNSW (1964), the extensions to the Supreme Court at Taylor Square (1963), and the New Wing (1963) to Registrar General, Queen's Sq, building in the city. All were designed by Peter Hall whilst in the Government Architect's Branch. Wood retired from PWD in June 1966 and moved to 8 Outram Street, West Perth, W.A., opposite King Park; registered as an architect in W.A. on 2 May 1967, in 1970 struck off for non–payment; he died early in 1976.

APR 24   Utzon sells his Bayview land Lot 1, D.P. 224856 at Mona Vale to solicitor **Frederick Mclure Edgington**.

✉ **APR 27**   Shopping Centre at Mona Vale, 12–14 Waratah Street, Mona Vale. 3 schemes for 10, 12 & 16 units for client, solicitor F.M. Edgington, Alexandra Cres. BAYVIEW.

APR 28   Cahill's successor, R.J. Heffron, resigns the Premiership in favour of **John (Jack) Brophy Renshaw** (b. 1909 –), insisting that 'nobody is throwing me out' over the budget issues of state aid to non–government schools and a means tested allowance of £21 a year to parents of children enrolled from 3rd year at Catholic and independent schools. His term as NSW Premier lasted 12 months till 12 May 1965. Renshaw was born at Wellington in western NSW, and later served as Treasurer in the Wran Labor government (1976 –).

MAY 4   Mr. R.W. Askin, Leader of the Opposition, questions the government's estimate of cost and suggests it will be more like A£18 M ($36 M).

3.00 p.m.: Meeting at Utzon's office to discuss hanging points from octopus arches to suspend radial hall beams.

MAY 17   Utzon absent from office for several weeks.

Minister for Works Ryan instructs Utzon that the new cost estimates NOT be divulged.

MAY 27   Results of Zurich competition are announced: 1st Utzon, 30,000 Fr (A£3,000); 2nd Angelo Cassoni, 18,000 Fr; 3rd Rudolf + Esther Guyer; 4th Kurt Zuger, 13,000 Fr. The scheme was drawn by Mogens Prip–Buus.The design was selected from 97 entries received by Zurich Council which ran the competition. The National Opera, Madrid, international competition was organised by the Juan March Foundation and judged by Egon Eiermann, Gio Ponti, Pierre Vago. Utzon's scheme failed to get a mention out of the 100 submitted. Results Pub: *L'arch. d'auj. hui*, no. 116, Sep./Nov.

MAY 27   Nutsch summarises acoustic situation: Minor Hall is acoustically functional; Major Hall remains problematical – further work on seating arrangement; necessary to form groups of listeners as per Berlin Philharmonic.

JUNE   Utzon returns in early June from Denmark following the death of his brother after 6 weeks absence from his Sydney office.

✉ Madrid Opera House (competition) drawn by Jon Lundberg and designed at boat shed is accompanied by a beautiful timber model. Situated on an island site in Madrid, it was inspired by ancient Egyptian temples, with walls all around edge, and a Bruce Goff like mast with suspension cable structure above the stage.

✉ **JUNE 10**   State Theatre complex, Zürich (competition) 1st prize. Utzon is notified by cable late May and by letter on June 10. He and his colleagues worked on it for fun as a hobby for six months in their spare time in Sydney. The jury praised the lucidity of the concept, the quality of the atmosphere in the auditorium, and the ability to add to the structure in the future which it thought would be inevitable. The Zürich press warmly greeted the jury's decision.

JUNE 16	SOHEC meeting #74: Utzon presents his ideas on (a) The Opera House and Circular Quay (b) Car Parking (d) Farm Cove Crescent Area (e) City Area and Pedestrian Ways (f) Trade Centre and indicates that it would be good for Sydney to have an overall development scheme. Pat Hills wags his finger at Utzon and admonishes, 'keep your nose out of our business.'
JUNE 18	Utzon gives new £A17.4 M estimate and completion date of December 1965. **Walter Bunning** calls for a Royal Commission.
JUNE 19	Premier Renshaw demands that Utzon to give him detailed explanation of rising costs and personally conducts an inquiry.
JUNE 21	By 31 March 1964, total unspent credit is A£3,843,529/0/7 in the Opera House account after 97 Opera House lotteries which raised £11 million.
JUNE 25	Utzon praises Nutsch's Sydney work to Cremer.
JUNE 30	SOHEC meeting, Utzon presents his proposal with schematic drawings for car parking alternatives.
	Fees paid to Utzon now total: A£431,289.3.9 ($862,578.00)
JULY	**First Australian military adviser killed in action in South Vietnam.**
JULY	Utzon family moves from Bayview to 65 Pacific Road, PALM BEACH, which he rents for £25 ($50) per week and leases the boat shed in Iluka Street a few months later from Godard family.
JULY 3	Meeting to discuss Executive Committee approval of Utzon's car parking station scheme.
JULY 15	**First issue of The Australian newspaper published by Rupert Murdock from Canberra, as a national daily newspaper challenging the duopoly of Fairfax and Packer publishing empires in Sydney.**
	New drawing of Main Hall auditorium by Jon Lundberg incorporating Cremer's requirements.
JULY 23	Thursday 11 a.m. Conference at the Premier's Department of Sub–committee consisting of the Deputy Premier and Minister for Local Government Mr. P.D. Hills, Minister for Public Works, Mr. P.N. Ryan, and Minister for Lands Mr. K.C. Compton with J. Utzon, Maclurcan, Prip–Buus, Nielsen present. Premier Renshaw challenges Utzon's estimate of A£17.4 million at a 90 minute meeting between Utzon and a cabinet sub–committee.
	Utzon says to Premier Renshaw that neither the latest estimate of A£17.4 million nor the completion date were meant for publication. Permission refused by Renshaw to table the parking station scheme. Renshaw, Hills and Ryan insist that the Minister for PWD is the client and no cost increase will be tolerated and it was up to the constructing authority to get the building completed within the financial limits imposed by Parliament. Mr Renshaw points out that the ceiling figure depends on the Parliament's approval.

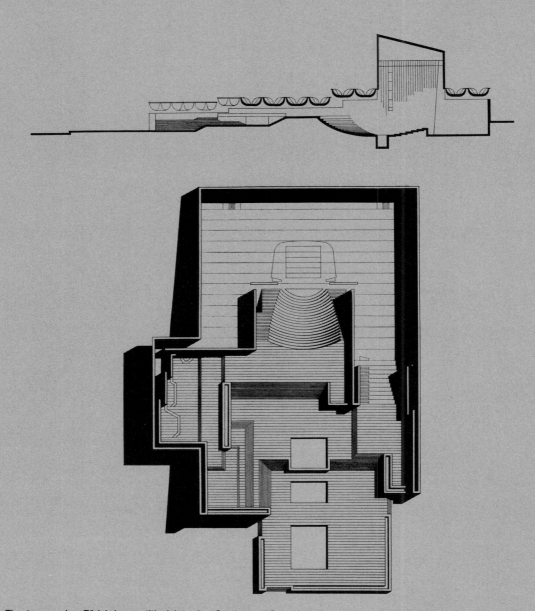

State Theatre complex, Zürich (competition) 1st prize. Section and floor plan.

AUG 4	Utzon forwards 1/8in scale models of interiors of Minor & Major Halls to Cremer in Berlin.
AUG 11	Utzon in Zürich, Switzerland, till 18th Aug, travels on to Berlin. Utzon later opened an office in Zürich.
AUG 22	Utzon visits Berlin and confers with his acoustical experts until 30 August.
AUG 20	Dean Dixon, musical director of Sydney Symphony Orchestra, inspects SOH site for first time with the manager of the orchestra Mr E. Gibb.
SEPT 15	Utzon reports to SOHEC at 34th Trust meeting about his meeting with Cremer, Gabler, Jordan and Nutsch and promises testing of acoustic model for Minor Hall will be completed by November 1964, and the Major Hall, by January 1965.
SEPT 18	Utzon submits plan for the redevelopment of Sydney Cove area.
SEPT 23	Utzon writes to Prof. Lothar Cremer to ask him to take over as engineering consultant for the electro–acoustics.
SEPT 29	Utzon writes to PWD Minister on the absolute necessity to engage Ralph Symonds Ltd to carry out the plywood engineering, structures, including erecting those structures.
OCT 7	Meeting held in Utzon's office with O. Arup, J. Zunz, M. Lewis, Utzon, O. Nielsen, M. Prip–Buus, R. Maclurcan to decide arrangements for completing Stage III work: Utzon to be responsible for geometry, physical dimensions of all elements — glass wall mullions, cladding, paving; OA & P to be responsible for structures of the elements only.
OCT 23	Arup and Jack Zunz arr. Sydney, stay at Belverdere Hotel, 81 Bayswater Road, Kings Cross.
OCT 25	New model of SOH put on display at David Jones store from Oct 26–Nov 30.
OCT 26	Design Meeting no. 1 held in Utzon's office: discusses glass walls.
OCT LATE	Utzon shifts design activity from Benelong Point office to Goddard's Boat Shed ground floor rear of shop at 118 Iluka Rd on Snapperman Beach, Palm Beach; he takes Prip–Buus, Lundberg, and Nayman, Richard Le Plastrier with him. Work at Bennelong Point office slows to a standstill, Frank D'Arcy, Ray Brownell, and Sergio Buzzolini leave. The boat shed conversion work was entrusted to Sergio Buzzolini. Rick Le Plastrier picks up after Buzzolini and starts work on the Bayview house from the boat shed. Frank D'Arcy resigns and leaves on Oct. 30.
OCT 29	Utzon is made a Fellow of R.A.I.A. (registered No. 4227).
OCT 29	10 a.m. meeting to discuss details of glass walls, OA & P request definition of total load factor of 60K required in the ceiling structure. Prip–Buus states that all drawings are now available and tables *SOH 1140-1141-1142-1143-1144-1145-1156-1147-1149-1150-1152-1153-1154-1155*, handed over to OA & P.
	Speaking in the debate on the Budget Estimates, Minister Ryan states on Oct. 28 that Utzon has not yet provided final estimate. (Utzon gave the minister the estimate 4 months earlier on June 18).

NOV 5   Utzon returns from overseas for TAP meet # 48 on 5 November 1964.

NOV   Design office moves to Palm Beach; Utzon takes Prip–Buus, Lundberg, Nayman along with him.

NOV 10   Lothar Cremer advises auditorium shells in two shells total load of 60 Kg/m², walls 100 kg/m².

NOV 16   Design Meeting no. 4

NOV 20   Utzon designs new medal for the national President of R.A.I.A. — *'new medal is being fitted and will be ready shortly.'*

NOV 23   Design Meeting no. 5 to discuss stage workshops, electric lifts, waterproofing basements.

NOV LATE   first consignment of stage machinery costing £1.6 million (A$3.2 M) leaves Europe by sea — announcement by Mr Walter Sedlaczek, sales manager of Waagner–Biro, Vienna.

NOV 26   Speaking in the Legislative Assembly on Nov. 25, Premier Renshaw says the Government would not accept a final estimate by Utzon, and Mr Ryan submits a series of questions to Utzon.

NOV 30   Design Meeting no. 6 to discuss structural tests on plywood carried out 20 Nov.

DEC 3   State Liberal Party's Opera House committee consisting of R.O. Healey (Wakehurst), I.R. Griffiths (Cronulla), and M. Morris (Maitland) visits SOH site.

Deadlock between City Council and State Government over parking.

DEC 7   Design Meeting no. 7: Utzon explains client's reasons for delaying signing Contract for stage III, mentions difficulty surrounding approval of Nominated Sub–Contractors.

DEC 11   J. Raffael (OA & P) reports tests on plywood beams are successful.

DEC 21   Monday: The first model of the proposed interior of the SOH put on display in Dept of Public Works built by Finecraft Scale Models Pty Ltd. The 1 inch to 8 ft scale model showed the cast and scenery of Act II of *Tosca* and took 14 months and cost A£5,000.

Seating capacity in Main Hall is now 2,800.

DEC   Christmas Party is held at the Music Hall, Neutral Bay.

Plans for Utzon's house at the end of Kara Crescent, BAYVIEW, Sydney, are rejected by Warringah Shire Council. Utzon paid $12,000 for Lot 2, D.P. 27991. Most of his spare time over a period of about 13 months went into designing the house. Four schemes were developed with Richard le Plastrier who assisted in the later stages.

Bill Wheatland sold the land in 1966 on Utzon's behalf.

Utzon rented a house in Ebor Road an outlying suburb of Palm Beach which previously belonged to the late Jim Banks, creator of Ginger Meggs. In the city, Utzon bought 18 Windsor Street, Paddington — he never lived in the house. Bill Wheatland was living there in 1966. The Paddington dwelling was owned by SISU Pty Ltd (1965), a company Utzon set up to market his furniture designs. The word is Finnish and means spiritual toughness, strength, or 'the final effort'.

BAYVIEW HOUSE, 1964 – 1965

1964

FEB	Scheme 1.
5 MAR	plans submitted by Sergio Buzzolini, a Swiss architect working in the office.
3 MAR	structural detail submitted.
16 APR	Utzon outlines the principles in letter to council.
NOV	Scheme 2. revised proposal submitted to WSC.
DEC 23	approved in principle.

1965

MAY	further documentation lodged by Le Plastrier.
JUNE 22	Scheme 3. drawings resubmitted.
DEC 17	Scheme 4. final Development Application lodged by Le Plastrier.
DEC 23	final approval

1965

Jørn & Lis holiday on Mallorca and he buys land on the coast near Porto Petro, including a second site in the southern Sierra del Levante mountains behind Alqueria Blanca. In 1970 he built his Can Lis house on the cliff at Colonia del Silencia, and later, after 1991, his Can Feliz house which was below an old Moorish castle at its back.

Jordan writes from Copenhagen to Utzon; model tests of Major Hall completed in early January.

JAN 11 Utzon registers a new subdivision no. 6180 for Lots 1,2,3 D.P. 27991 at Kara Crescent, Bayview, in Parish of Narrabeen created as D.P. 224856 under Torrens Title. Previous D.P. for land was D.P. 4010 and 27991. The total area is 5a. 3r. 11.5p. plus Lot 62 on adjoining west boundary

JAN 18 Design Meeting no. 9 to discuss structure for Halls: Utzon presents preliminary structural design drawings of wall and ceiling structures of Major and Minor Halls and preliminary structural design drawings of glass walls.

JAN 25 Design Meeting no. 10.

FEB 2	Design Meeting no. 11 to discuss the Engineer's report on design of the Major Hall ceiling, balconies, galleries, seating, Major Hall ceiling, glass walls etc.
FEB 4	NSW Parliament prorogued till March 16.
FEB 8	**Shirley Colless** starts work as Utzon's secretary in Bennelong Point office.
FEB 9	Mr P.N. Ryan says final cost and date of completion of SOH is to be announced before the end of the year.
FEB 12	Design Meeting no. 12 to discuss Engineer's Progress Report.
FEB 22	Design Meeting no. 13 to discuss CSIRO Report on plywood durability tests.
MAR 11	Meeting at Utzon's Benelong Point office on acoustic schemes.
MAR 18	Design Meeting no. 15.
MAR 22	Design Meeting no. 16: Engineer's Report on glass walls, cladding & paving, skirting, canopies Major & Minor Halls.
MAR 23	Meeting at Utzon's office to discuss plywood and manufacture of glass wall mullions, choice of white seraya versus coachwood.
MAR 24	Design Meeting no. 17: plywood durability tests carried forward from March 18 meeting.
APR 5	Monday evening: Leader of the Country Party in NSW, C.B. Cutler, delivers the party policy speech to launch campaign at Orange; 150 attend, including Askin.
APR 8	Design Meeting no. 18.
APR	Strikes at SOH site.
APR 12	Utzon is away overseas for six weeks in Berlin to supervise acoustic tests on April 20, returns before 23 May.
APR 21	**Alex Popov** and Lin Utzon meet at B.Arts graduation party in January. Popov studied Arts/Psychology (1961–1964) and was editor of *Tharunka* (UNSW student paper) before Richard Neville took over in 1964.
APR 22	Design Meeting no. 19.
MAY	**Australian combat troops are sent to participate in the Vietnam War.**
	Utzon completes comparison of plywood suppliers for Stage III and concludes that Ralph Symonds is the only firm with the requisite production and testing facilities to satisfy quality standards
MAY 1	**State Poll — Labor Party defeated. Election result is close and the fate of the Labor Government was not known for about 10 days. Liberal: 31 seats; Country Party: 16 seats (Total 47 seats to A.L.P. 45 seats); Independents: 2 seats; The Monaro electorate decided the election outcome. In Sydney A.L.P. won 28 seats to Liberal 19, Independent 1.**
MAY 3	Design Meeting no. 20
	Mrs Utzon is rushed into hospital.

MAY 5	Utzon in Berlin observing acoustical consultants; test model of the Minor Hall very successful, minor adjustments required to Major Hall.
MAY 6	Meeting to discuss structural design of elements of stage III.
MAY 10	Design Meeting no. 21
MAY 13	**Sir Robert Askin takes office as Premier of NSW while Utzon is out of Australia.**
MAY 17	Design Meeting no. 22
MAY 23	Meeting at Engineer's office at 2.30 p.m.: Utzon submits three alternative schemes for minimum use of plywood for auditoria; Lewis favours (c) *SOH 1408, 1380*.
	Utzon, who has been away since April 12, returns from Europe
MAY 30	Jon Lundberg resigns and leaves Australia and returns to Denmark and begins his own practice, while assisting on the Zürich Theatre project.
JUNE 1	Utzon sends letter to Minister requesting approval of Ralph Symonds Ltd for plywood glass walls.
	Utzon sells land Lot 3, D.P. 224856 at Bayview to Gervaise Churchill, a photographer.
JUNE 3	Thursday: farewell party for Olaf Skipper–Nielsen who returns to Århus in Denmark via New Delhi, Chandigarh, Moscow.
JUNE 6	Wednesday: Hughes and Utzon discuss parking and improvements to the surrounds of the SOH area.
JUNE 10	Meeting at Utzon's office to refine the plywood mullions; Utzon's office has for last three months been working on an alternative structure for the mullions based on the pipe idea. Reports on acoustical consultation work in Berlin and the success of model tests of the two halls.
JUNE 10	Utzon comes into the office and walks across the floor on his hands to celebrate the hollow pipe solution of the mullions.
JUNE 16	Meeting between Hughes and Utzon.
JUNE 18	**Mr R.A.P. Johnson** (former Director of PWD) retires.
JUNE 21	Utzon submits *Report on Acoustical Research on Major and Minor Halls, Sydney Opera House, June 1965* (ordered by previous Minister for Public Works, P.N. Ryan) which sets out in detail the stages in the design of the two principal halls.
	Wednesday: meeting between Utzon — including R. Maclurcan, W. Wheatland and M. Prip–Buus from his office — and Hughes, Mr R.A.P. (Alan) Johnson (Director of PWD) and W.W. Wood
JUNE 23–25	NSW Annual conference of the Australian Country Party at Wagga Wagga.
JULY	**National Service conscription by birthday lottery is introduced.**

JULY 1
Meeting at Utzon's office, the architect tables draw nos. *SOH 1222, 1223* set out and *1229, 1230–1238* showing the principles and details for the new glass wall structure based on plywood pipe structure.

JULY 10
Opening night of Sutherland–Williamson International Grand Opera Company Tour at Her Majesty's Theatre, Melbourne, featuring Joan Sutherland in *Lucia di Lammermoor* by Donizetti. The company includes Luciano Pavarotti, John Alexander, Lauris Elms, Robert Allman, Margreth Elkins and Clifford Grant.

JULY 15
Meeting in Utzon's office at 11 p.m. on glass walls: Utzon explains that the final geometry for the south glass wall depends solely on detailed mock–ups that there will be only a slight divergence from the last drawing made. Engineers advise that they do not consider bending or stability tests are necessary.

JULY 16
Co–ordination and Pre–planning Meeting no. 7 SOH Stage III. Permission still awaited approving Symonds.

JULY 21
Wed: discussions between Utzon, Maclurcan, Wheatland, Buus from his office and D. Hughes, Johnson (Director PWD), W.W. Humphrey & W.W. Wood on parking for 1,000 cars, plywood contractor Mr R. Symonds, revised estimate by quantity surveyors Rider Hunt & Partners A£24.2 million which Utzon amends to A£24.7 million to allow for contingencies and acoustics.

JULY 28
Meeting at Dept of PWD at 12.15 p.m. requested by R.A.P. Johnson (Director PWD) to discuss definition of Symond's work, prototypes of mullions and auditorium ceiling. Critical meeting for Utzon with Mr Esra & Mr Fellew of Ralph Symonds Ltd present; D. Hughes is absent.

AUG 5
Utzon reports results of acoustic tests on large scale models in Berlin & Copenhagen confirm latest shapes. At August meeting of SOHEC Utzon's claim for £12,000 ($24,000) is passed for payment.

AUG 10–20
Jørn, Lis & Kim go on holidays to Heron Island, off Gladstone, North Queensland for at least 10 days. Heron Island is less than 1 km long and has a resort and a research station on it. Meet Milton Moon (an Adelaide potter). Utzon later wrote a letter of support for Moon's Churchill Fellowship in 1965.

AUG 10
Tuesday: discussion between Hughes, S. Haviland, J. Humphrey on relationship between Minister and the SOH Trust, SOHEC; subject of professional fees paid to Consultants is raised.

AUG 11
W.W. Wood (PWD Liaison Architect) meets Davis Hughes to discuss measures to control SOH project.

AUG 12
W.W. Wood writes confidential memo to Davis Hughes in which he outlines four measures to be adopted including control of Utzon by application of 'cheque book control' to withhold fees and the establishment of a drafting office.

AUG 17
Arrival of stage machinery from Europe worth £370,000; weighs 350 tons. Last seen in a field at Silverwater off Silverwater Road in its original packing cases. It was later sent to Old Sydney Town at Gosford on the Central Coast.

AUG 22
Utzon returns after 20 August from Heron Island holiday.

AUG 24
Mr D. Hughes promises in the Legislative Assembly that work on SOH will continue.

Rolling cylinder profile for auditorium ceiling.

AUG 25   Mr D. Hughes has lunch with **Mr R. Gilling**, President of NSW Chapter RAIA, at the Pioneers' Club–Australasian, 61 York Street, Sydney 2000. In *Hansard*, claimed that E.H. Farmer and Director PWD were present. Gilling refers to only Mr. J.C. Humphrey. After the lunch Gilling talked to Mr. C.J. Farrington, Immediate Past President of the Chapter.

Hughes writes a confidential Cabinet Minute seeking the approval of Cabinet to implement 7 measures, and in particular 1 & 7, in the knowledge they could lead to a dispute with the architect. (7) involves the application of a reducing scale fee for Utzon's work. Hughes also writes to Utzon on basic principles that must govern construction.

AUG 26   R. Gilling and R. Maclurcan have first official interview with the Minister Mr Davis Hughes.

Gilling does not inform Utzon following this meeting.

AUG 28   Wednesday: Hughes visits Bennelong Point and is shown around by Utzon; discussion in site office follows.

AUG 29   Utzon sacks Robert Maclurcan for conspiring with Gilling and Hughes.

AUG 30   Tuesday: Minister announces the new cost estimate of A£24.7 million pounds ($49.4 M) and pushes completion date forward from 1967 to 1969.

Fees and expenses paid Utzon at end of August amount to A£547,553 ($1,095,106), bringing total amount paid to consultants A£1,495,422 ($2,990,844).

That same day, Utzon writes inviting Gilling to lunch at Bennelong Point offices 'to put you in the picture as you have had a meeting with the Minister for Public Works about the Opera House.'

Davis Hughes prepares to make a Ministerial Statement to the NSW Parliament then cancels at last moment.

SEPT–OCT   **Prof. Steen Eiler Rasmussen,** Utzon's former teacher, whom Utzon encouraged to come to Australia, lectures at UNSW. His approach is quiet and low key; asks students questions and stimulates them to think.

SEPT   Utzon family moves to cnr. Ebor & Cynthea Roads, PALM BEACH, on the return from overseas of the Pacific Road house owner.

SEPT 1   Mr A.E. Armstrong, a government member in the L–CP Coalition, calls for suspension of work and setting up of a Royal Commission of Inquiry.

SEPT 2   Utzon works on changes to the ceiling profile of the Major Hall.

SEPT 3   Friday: Meeting between Hughes, Utzon, Humphrey at Parliament House at which Hughes asserts his role as Client; refers to financial position viz a viz lotteries; Symonds issue raised. Utzon indicates architectural drawings well advanced; invites Colin Humphrey, Woods, Jones, McConnel to inspect drawings, and is asked to prepare schedule of works with dates of completion.

SEPT 9   Gilling replies to Utzon's lunch invitation of 31 August.

SEPT 22	Wednesday: meeting between Hughes, Haviland, and Director PWD at Parliament House; concern expressed at lack of drawings for Stage III; review of the scale of fees paid to Utzon as project now under the control of Minister, agrees future payments by PWD. Role of Trust/Committee to advise Utzon on request but Minister's approval is required for adoption of any proposal. SOH Executive Committee was not informed by the previous Minister (Ryan) of the A£17.4 million estimate.
SEPT 23	Gilling has lunch with Utzon but makes no attempt to familiarise himself with Opera House work in a visit which lasted 2 hours.
SEPT 27	Meeting at office of Minister between Hughes, J.C. Humphrey, S. Haviland, Prof H.I. Ashworth and Utzon to discuss use of network analysis to manage production of architectural drawings for Stage III. Utzon responds: all drawings will be ready within 12 months but admits there are problems with certain major items including glass walls and auditoria which are dependent on agreement over the production of plywood mock–ups. Gives staffing levels as 16 in Sydney, 3 in Denmark (total 19), and plans to hire 4 more in one month's time. Completion date is now set as late 1969. Utzon requests authority to proceed with construction of plywood mock–ups.
SEPT 28	Utzon lodges claim for £24,000 ($48,000) in fees to be paid immediately to the SOH Executive Committee.
OCT 1	Utzon submits a schedule for completion of documents to Minister, sent to Minister on 11 October.
OCT 8	Friday: NSW government reveals rise in cost of the roof of A£1.8 million. Davis Hughes assumes personal control over the costs of the project.
OCT 15	Friday: Utzon offer to show Hughes, W.W. Wood and Mr R.A.P. Johnson material prepared by Concrete Industries for paving and cladding.
	Utzon submits a statement of fees owing of £24,000 ($48,000), previously submitted to SOH Executive Committee without result.
OCT 19	SOHEC meeting: under minute 'Account' an entry 'NIL' appears beside Utzon's fees.
OCT 22	Utzon in Berlin at Berlin Institute for Acoustics Laboratory with Profs Cremer & Gabler.
	Leaves Berlin for Sydney in the company of Mr Nutsch. Roger Clovell inspects model and writes article.
OCT 27	Wednesday: Davis Hughes takes over responsibility for payments to Utzon from the Dept. of Local Government and stops payments.
	Pop concert given by The Easy Beats, and party at SOH site, 350 people attended. Party arranged by a 25 year old journalist **Jilian (Jill) Robertson** (b. 1940–), **Lin Utzon** in attendance. Thunder storm at sunset ends the party.
OCT 28	Utzon submits claim for £51,626 ($103, 252) for the stage machinery work done in 1960.

NOV 1 Monday: disagreement with M.Lewis (OA & P): Utzon writes to Lewis that he, Utzon, has not received a reply about his submission on the design of the auditoria sent August 27.

Utzon again writes to Hughes regarding the £24,000 payment of outstanding fees on account and questions the behaviour of M. Lewis, who gave his advice directly to Minister and by-passed Utzon in his role as Architect responsible for consultants.

NOV 3 Wednesday: Ministerial Statement by Minister Hughes in the Legislative Assembly; submits a detailed report and attacks previous Labour management of the project (See *Hansard* No. 28, 41st Parliament–2nd Session, pp. 1690–1732).

NOV 4 Thursday: Hughes presents car parking proposal to Mr Askin. The details are withheld.

NOV 8 Monday: meeting between Wheatland, Mr. Walker (PWD secretary) in connection with the fees dispute.

NOV 9 Tuesday: Utzon writes again on the matter of the £24,000 ($48,000) in fees owing. A meeting is held between Utzon, Wood and Lloyd covering fees; in a letter he encloses a revised statement of fees as per discussion.

NOV 11 Thursday: Secretary Lloyd writes enclosing cheque for the £24,000 ($48,000).

NOV 15 Monday: Utzon replies expressing concern that the amount is based on payment for future not executed services already delivered.

NOV 17 Executive Committee meeting no. 79, Utzon reveals he has already paid £7,000 to Ralph Symonds Ltd personally for work on the glass walls.

NOV 19 Friday: meeting between Hughes, J.C. Humphrey, T.H. Walker, S. Haviland, Prof Ashworth, Utzon at which Utzon describes experiments with fixing tile lids and announces arrival of Mr Nutsch on Monday 29 November. Lengthy discussion of Stage III, in particular glass wall mullions and construction of the auditoria. M. Lewis to leave Sydney in mid–December.

NOV 29 Meeting in Utzon's office 10 a.m. to 12.30 p.m., to discuss progress on Stage III, Hughes, Humphrey, R. A.P. Johnson, Walker, & Nutsch present: discussion of Minor Hall and acoustics, stage technique, cladding & paving; Prof. L. Cremer's Report from Berlin is tabled. 2 p.m. meeting at Utzon's office follows on re–location of Leonard transformer room.

DEC 2 Meeting in Engineer's office: Utzon tables draw. *SOH 803–835–841–842*; explains his scheme and asks Engineer to give his opinion on desirability of using steel and plywood of maximum size 9ft x 50ft.

DEC 17 Meeting between Hughes, J.C. Humphrey, T.H. Walker, S. Haviland, Prof Ashworth and Utzon: Technical Panel had discussed motion supporting Utzon's request to proceed with mock–ups; Utzon asks for clarification on his position re. the Engineer; Lewis unable to complete his report on plywood in time; question raised about future social functions at Bennelong Point raised and a Management Committee meeting weekly set up.

DEC 23 Meeting in Engineer's office discusses cladding, finishes, fixings, erection, glass walls; draw nos. *SOH 1386–1385–1341–1340–1320–1319–1318–1312–1307–1294–1293–1292–1291*.

Office Christmas party held at Villa Franca Restaurant, 346 Liverpool Street, Paddington; the restaurant closed immediately afterwards. Food did not arrive till 11 p.m., Nutsch commented: *'thought it was going to be a riot.'* Utzon did not attend.

DEC 24 <u>Fee of £20,000 ($40,000) received by Utzon</u>; he leaves for Japan the following day accompanied by Lis and Kim.

DEC 25 Utzon departs for Japan and Hawaii; visits Tokyo and Nara; Jan and Lin Utzon had left earlier and stay for an extended period of three months in Japan.

1965 University Art Museum, Berkeley, California (competition).

1966

JAN Utzon is on holidays and visits Japan and Hawaii to study the problem of acoustics in relation to the use of plaster ceilings — later he states that he is satisfied the use of plaster is undesirable.

JAN 5 Meeting in Engineer's (OA & P) office to discuss drawing nos. *SOH 1112/SK/S239* 'Minor Hall Auditorium Ceiling Webs Detail'.

JAN 10 Utzon's staff return to work.

JAN 17 Meeting in Engineer's office discusses erection joints, construction joints in plywood ceiling; Minor Hall ceiling discussed — re question of ½ inch or 1 inch plywood panels; Nutsch to advise — reverberation times will dictate sizes.

JAN 18 *SOH 1393*: Major Hall Section. Models are made of *SOH 1392 f* scheme for Major Hall with increased volume following the discovery of Lundberg's mistake in locating 'line of safety' zone.

JAN 18 Meeting in Engineer's office to discuss cladding & paving drawings.

JAN 19 Jørn, Lis and Kim staying at the Nara Hotel, Nara Park, Japan.

JAN 25 John G. Nutt submits *Report on the Structural Details of the Proposed Scheme for the Minor Hall Auditoria Ceiling* to Utzon and writes to Director of PWD.

JAN 26 **Sir Robert Menzies retires on Australia Day after 17 years as Prime Minister (19 Dec. 1949 – 1966).**

JAN 26 Lothar Cremer sends Utzon a telegram congratulating him on the acoustics solution of Major Hall *SOH draw. 1392 f*. This final scheme was never model tested, however, it was geometrically confirmed by Nutsch.

FEB 1 The Utzon's stay at Honolulu, Hawaii. Utzon is a partner with **Peer Abben** in architectural firm specialising in commercial work, blocks of flats etc., mentioned.

1966

ABBEN

Peer Abben, was a former class mate from the Royal Academy. Abben was born Sep. 8, 1916, completed architectural studies in 1943 and was registered A.I.A. at 677 Ala Moana Boulevard, Suite 913 A, Honolulu, USA 961815, Hawaii.

FEB 8 Utzon returns to Sydney from Hawaii. During the first week, Utzon confides to M. Lewis he is considering resigning. Lewis suggests that Utzon employ Peddle Thorp & Walker to do working drawings

FEB 10 Utzon presents a model of the restaurant showing an interior on four levels to the Tec. Advis. Panel illustrating its functions and layout. The same day he writes to Ove Arup saying he engaged OA personally; the crisis is similar to situation which arose with scrapping of 1st scheme for the shells; the behaviour of the OA & P's Sydney office is unprofessional.

FEB 14 Monday: Utzon writes to Secretary PWD that the plywood report by Nutt is not based on firm calculations or refinement of the structure. Utzon forwarded his comments in a report on *Comments on Report Presented by Messrs. Ove Arup & Partners, Engineers, January 1966, Concerning Structure of the Minor Hall Auditorium Ceiling, Sydney Opera House.*

FEB 15 Tuesday: Utzon writes to Hughes about the urgency of a decision on plywood mock–ups and justifies the nature of the proposal in a lengthy report. In the run–up to removing Utzon, Davis Hughes telephones senior newspaper editors daily to appraise them of the position re SOH and wins John Pringle at the *SMH* over to the idea that Utzon has to go, despite the presence there of George Molnar as cartoonist.

FEB 18 Friday: Michael Lewis, left for London before 20 January and returned to Sydney on Feb. 18. In London, he and Zunz reviewed Dr John Nutt's report on the Minor Hall ceiling structure before it was sent to Utzon.

Meeting between Hughes, J.C. Humphrey, T.H. Walker, S. Haviland, Prof Ashworth, W.W. Wood and Utzon, at which Utzon reported on his overseas trip, early completion of restaurant is discussed, investigation of an organ, naming the halls, critical path schedule and plywood for the auditoria ceilings. Minister stated that the Engineer's disagreed with Mr Utzon on the plywood proposal. Utzon had spoken earlier to them and they had agreed to withdraw their report.

Meeting at Bennelong Point chaired by W.W. Wood, the purpose of which is to recommend work to be done in the interim between end of Stage II Contract and start of Stage III.

FEB 24 Drawing no. *SOH 1452*: Major Hall Sections through Ceiling Panels, completed and a model was made on Feb 28 after Nutsch left.

Meeting with ABC officers and SOH Trust members: W.J. Mehaffey criticises Major Hall's acoustic deficiencies as venue for SSO — noise, seating, acoustics, inadequately sized rehearsal rooms.

FEB 26   Saturday: Shirley Colless (Utzon's personal secretary) drives to the Utzon's Palm Beach house and is informed by Mr and Mrs Utzon of a [dire financial] situation and what was likely to happen.

On this visit, she brings the 2 copies of the accounts made at Lis Utzon's request, Lis and Jørn Utzon tell her that he is facing an enormous tax bill by Commonwealth Tax Office as he has already been taxed in Denmark. To pay this he will either have to reach a settlement with the Australian Government or sell up and leave the country.

FEB 28   Monday: Utzon withdraws from the SOH project under pressure by **Davis Hughes**. Utzon has meeting with Hughes at 12.00 noon at which Minister refused to pay certain fees which had been owing since 1961. Letter delivered to Hughes by Shirley Colless to Minister's Secretary at 3.00 p.m. that afternoon. Hughes telephones M. Lewis and Corbett Gore on Monday afternoon to say it is his intention to accept Utzon's resignation. News of Utzon resignation is first broadcast on 10 o'clock news on ABC Radio. Hughes' reply is sent announces Utzon's 'resignation' is held on Monday night to guarantee the story is run in the press next morning. Utzon ignored Bill Wheatland and Shirley Colless' advice to consult a solicitor first before submitting the letter. Ron Gilling is contacted at 11.30 p.m. by *Daily Telegraph* reporter wishing to confirm story of Utzon's resignation.

> ## HUGHES
>
> Davis Hughes b. 24 Nov. 1910, m. Joan Philip Johnson July 6, 1940, Educated Launceston High School, Tasmania; Phillip Smith Teachers College, Hobart, Tas; Teacher, Tasmania, Friends' School, Hobart, served during war sqdn ldr RAAF, Australia and overseas, 1940–45 as an instructor in navigation; Mayor of Armidale, 1953–56; Armidale representative for Farmers and Graziers, works his electorate in preparation of elections, MLA NSW 1950–53 and 1956–65; Leader of NSW Country Party 1958–59 (resigned leadership), in March–April 1959 during State elections he disappears, later relinquishes Leadership of C.P., and apologises for misleading Parliament, Minister for Public Works, NSW, 1965–73, 1968 becomes Deputy Leader of C.P. under Charles Cutler, appointed Agent General for NSW in London, and leaves before SOH is opened in Feb. 1973.

MARCH 1   Tuesday: journalists camp outside Utzon's Palm Beach house at 7.30 a.m.

Prip–Buus and Wheatland to go to 89 Jersey Road, Paddington where Utzon is (temporary home of Jan & Lin); Union jack hanging from veranda; the three go for a walk in Centennial Park; return to discuss options. Peer Abben turns up at the house in the meantime, from Hawaii, and waits at the gate; he talks

UTZON SYDNEY OFFICE

Utzon's Sydney office is disbanded; staff includes Mogens Prip–Buus, Oktay Nayman (both worked with Utzon at Hellebæk), Nayman's Australian wife, Paul Hopkins (working on the plywood structures and glass walls), Mary Wilson (working on the major and minor Halls) Michael Tomaszewski (cladding and paving), Clive Buhrich, Peter Myers (experimental theatre), and Peter Campagnoni.

about Kenzo Tange (Airport terminal); Paul Rudolph meeting with the Sheik of Kuwait. Utzon decides to present 8 points to the Minister.

Hughes commences discussions on completion of SOH without Utzon. Issues a statement: *'Government will complete the Opera House.'*

Laurie Hegvold interviews Utzon at Wheatland's terrace house in Hargrave Street, Paddington, in the ground floor front room, early Tuesday morning for *The Architecture Club* (April 1966, issue) magazine, later interviews Peter Hall at his flat overlooking Lavender Bay and Hughes in his Ministerial Office.

5 p.m. Ashworth has meeting with the Minister in presence of Humphrey, Buus and Wheatland.

J.C. Humphrey, Director PWD, rings Gilling in morning to ask him to meet Hughes that day. 8 p.m. meeting at Minister's Office at Parliament House with Hughes, Humphrey, E.H. Farmer, C. Weatherburn, at which R. Gilling is informed by Hughes that Utzon has resigned. The same day, Gilling instructs **Milo Dunphy** (b. Brighton–le–Sands 13 May 1929–d. Sydney April 1996), RAIA Chapter Council's Public Relations Acting Chairman, to make no statement. Ron Gilling accepts Utzon's resignation at face value and supports the Minister's need for architectural services.

Utzon, Wheatland and Prip–Buus meet Davis Hughes Tuesday night at Parliament House and present list of 9 conditions to which Minister must agree for Utzon to return to the job. Hughes rejects 2, 4, 5, 6, 7, 8, does not appear to understand 9. Hughes described by Wheatland as looking very tired. Utzon gives Hughes an undertaking not to approach the press. The meeting ends at 7.30 p.m. Leaves through rear door of Parliament, returns to Bennelong Point to report to staff (15). Wheatland then drives Utzon to Palm Beach, Peer Abben stays there with family, 10 p.m. Reaches Paddington at 11.30 p.m.

MAR 2   Wednesday: 2.30 p.m.: Gilling talks on site for about one hour with Wheatland and Buus, and subsequently 20 minutes with Utzon. Utzon returns to site at 3 p.m. and Gilling offers the support of his Institute.

3.20 p.m.: Gilling meeting with Prof Ashworth, discuss Utzon's terms briefly.

THE SPRUCE GOOSE

It was conceived in 1942, on 1.30 p.m., Nov 2, 1947, and, at the Long Beach Channel, California, Howard Hughes' 350,000lb (158,760kg) Flying Boat flew for a brief 60 seconds. Built almost entirely of birch veneer wood using a manufacturing process called duramold, twice as large as anything in its day, it was the world's largest aircraft. Hughes first used the process in 1934 to construct the wings of his record–breaking H–1 racer. The veneers used in duramold were as thin as 1/32–inch in thickness. A small amount of metal was incorporated in its farings and the tube engine mounts, but the rest was made of laminated structural shapes formed in special moulds by a secret process which included steaming to produce the intricate shapes required. Its dimensions demonstrate Ove Arup and Partners timitidty in rejecting Utzon's plans for plywood auditoriums whose total weight was no more than the 200 tons of the flying boat which was 66.65m long compared to 67.06m for the Concert Hall and had a 97.53m wingspan and total height of 21.42m. The total weight of the Opera House roof vaults is an astonishing 157,800 tons, over four times the 37,000 tons of steel used in the 503m long arch of the Sydney Harbour Bridge. Utzon's proposed plywood vaults weighed a mere 1/785th of the concrete roofs.

3.30 p.m.: Gilling receives a deputation of some 25 architects led by Seidler and including Kevin Rice, requesting a positive statement on the Opera House dispute; Gilling in a change of heart offers Utzon the RAIA's support. Utzon arrives at close of meeting and gives Gilling a copy of the 9 points.

A 4 ton steel erection arch collapses and falls 30 ft from concert hall shell — no one is hurt.

4.30 p.m.: first meeting of RAIA Select Committee to consider how best to provide the Government with architectural services to complete the Sydney Opera House.

In a statutory Declaration, dated 28 March, Harry Seidler declares that he attended a select Committee meeting of the RAIA at Miller Street, NORTH SYDNEY. Soon after the start of this meeting, the President, Mr R. Gilling said words to this effect: *'The Minister of Public Works wants our help to suggest a panel of architects to complete the Opera House. We must give him this. What I envisage is a man with Utzon's spirit of design — Mr. B. Mortlock, someone to do the working drawings — Mr. O. Jarvis, because he worked on the Opera House plans in Denmark some years ago, and a firm to do the general administration — Edwards, Madigan & Torzillo, because they get along well with the Government Architects.'*

Ashworth meets Mr Haviland on his return from Bathurst. At 1700 hrs Ashworth meets with Minister Hughes, Haviland, Humphrey, Farmer. Farmer & Humphrey leave at 4.30 p.m. Director again raises take over arrangements for drawings and documents. Utzon gives Farmer a speech better than Socrates' speech to the Athenian Senate on the architect's ethical and design responsibilities, when offered the choice of dishonour or death and chose death.

Mr. O. Jarvis has a conversation with Utzon at night, comments that Utzon is still suspicious of the Institute following the Gilling–Hughes meeting in August. Utzon returns to office to report.

P.A. Dorrian at ABC to AGM, 'I think it would be wise for us not to be caught up in any activities in the planning and design of the interior which could subsequently lead to it being said we had even some indirect responsibility for it.'

MAR 3   Thursday, morning 10 a.m.: Select Committee together with Mr Seidler, meet at the Government Architect's office with E.H. Farmer and C. Weatherburn; the consortium is named to Seidler.

McShane, a clerk from PWD, comes to Utzon's office says Director and Farmer will visit to discuss the 'taking over arrangements.' Director telephones office and Utzon agrees to meet Farmer and Director at 3 p.m.

12 noon: Gilling meets Director Humphrey and briefly discusses what has transpired.

1 p.m.: architects and students march from the Opera House to Parliament House where a deputation puts Utzon's case to Premier R. Askin.

2.30 p.m.: Gilling talks to Hughes at Parliament House briefly who agrees to see Utzon.

3.30 p.m.: members of Select Committee (Hanson and Mortlock) inspect the site with Seidler.

Utzon returns to Palm Beach, has afternoon swim and holds discussions with Peer Abben before his return to Hawaii.

Phone call from Ove Arup to Utzon is treated with disdain.

5.00 p.m.: RAIA Committee meet, Gilling dismisses Milo Dunphy from all Council and Committee activities and Seidler from Select Committee meetings for attending march.

Mick Lewis asks Shirley Colless when Utzon will vacate the office.

Site visit, Seidler shown around by Oktay Nayman and Ron Devine. Office closes at 7 p.m.

Hughes flies to Armidale Thursday evening. Further talks suspended until Monday.

MAR 4   Friday: Utzon speaks to press.

9.00 a.m.: Committee meet: President Gilling writes to Minister stating that Mr Utzon 'should remain in full design control of the construction of the project.'

10.30 a.m.: Gilling makes statement to the press.

12 noon: Ashworth visits Opera House site and is met by Prip–Buus and Wheatland.

3 p.m.: Ashworth in the company of Mr Haviland (SOHEC). Ashworth rings Hughes in Tamworth to arrange a meeting early next week — agrees to Monday afternoon at Premier's Department.

Utzon arrives at 5.20 p.m. Meeting lasts to 6.45 p.m. Sets off in Ron Devine's Lancia up Macquarie St to Premier Askin's office. Mogens and Utzon are surrounded by reporters and go to waiting room where they encounter Ashworth and Haviland before seeing Premier Askin in his office. Utzon gives a report and copy of 9 points demands. Askin explains the political pressure the Minister is under from within the Country Party. Utzon says M. Lewis has rescinded his objection to structural soundness of ceiling scheme and the willingness of OA & P to collaborate further. Premier refers to 'loss of face' for Hughes. Utzon makes statement to reporters in Askin's presence — talks had been friendly, there were areas of difference. Walks back to OH accompanied by 2 Australian reporters and 1 Dane.

5.00 p.m.: Committee review position. Gilling telephones Humphrey who assures him no one in PWD is authorised to approach anyone to set up an architectural panel.

6.30 p.m. Gilling in press release RAIA rejects role of recommending an architects panel to Hughes.

MAR 5   Saturday: Utzon is supposed to have taken Peer Abben on drive in country that weekend —

really, to avoid press. Utzon was negotiating a contract to build a hotel in Hawaii with Abben.

MARCH 7   Monday: 11.15 a.m.: Gilling meets Hughes and Humphrey shown a copy of draft "Basis of Proposal" conditions for re-engagement of Utzon.

3 p.m.: Utzon, Wheatland and Mr M. Prip–Buus meet Davis Hughes at 3 p.m. in Mr Hughes' office. Also present are the Director of Public Works, Mr J.C. Humphrey, the Government Architect, Mr E.H. Farmer, Mr S. Haviland, Professor H. Ingham Ashworth for the Sydney Opera House Trust. Hughes tells Utzon his conditions, Utzon, Prip–Buus and Wheatland withdraw to adjoining veranda for 45 minutes to consider terms of offer, returns to office and discussion continues for another 90 minutes. Premier is unavailable at this time.

MAR 8   Tuesday: A day of talks by government confirms Utzon's removal from the SOH project.

9.45 a.m., Ashworth has long discussion with Premier Askin. He agrees with Prof Winston's request to convene a Technical Panel meeting but fails to do so afterwards.

2.00 p.m., message from Mr Haviland that Cabinet has decided to support action by Minister, Mr Hughes.

In the afternoon Utzon talks to Mr J.R. Renshaw and Mr P.N. Ryan at Parliament. Leaves Renshaw at 6p.m. to talk to reporters.

4.00 p.m.: Gilling makes a full report of all actions to RAIA Council, meeting adjourned at 10.30 p.m. after passing motion supporting Hughes' 'Basis of Proposal'.

10.30 p.m.: Gilling goes to Utzon's office, is initially refused admittance but is finally admitted on insistence of Max Collard at 11 p.m. Is accompanied by M.E. Collard, G.L. Moline, N.A. Ashton, B. Mortlock, D. Gazzard, M. Dunphy. Utzon has Seidler and Peter Miller with him in addition to Wheatland and Prip–Buus. At 11.15 p.m. Gilling telephones Hughes at Parliament to come down but Hughes refuses.

12.00 Midnight: Gilling & Mortlock call on Hughes at Parliament and argue that Utzon is competent.

1.30–3.00 a.m.: Gilling, Mortlock, Collard & Moline reconvene at Chapter and agree to try to persuade Utzon to see Hughes again.

MAR 9   Wednesday: 7.30 a.m., Gilling telephones P. Miller and asks him to persuade Utzon not to reject the Hughes proposal.

9.15 a.m.: Hughes telephones Gilling to enquire on progress in arranging another meeting.

A press statement by Utzon is published in the morning papers, '…no architect can compromise,'

Meanwhile, Hughes plans new team to take over.

In Questions without Notice (41st Parliament–2nd Session, Hansard No. 55, pp. 4008, 4019–4032) Mr Ryan attacks Hughes over Utzon's forced withdrawal from project.

Friends of the Opera House Committee established at Peter Kollar's house.

MAR 10   Thursday, 9.30 a.m.: Gilling issues a press release for RAIA as President of NSW Chapter.

9.30 a.m.: Wheatland talks briefly to Haviland.

10 a.m.: Utzon arrives at Bennelong Point, talks to Haviland about convening a meeting of SOH Trust & TAP; P. Miller and Seidler arrive and meet Utzon; Miller outlines a plan. Farmer rings, wanting to come to Benelong Point to take over — had a letter and instructions from Minister.

Utzon gives Harry Seidler a draft letter to send to the newspapers and promises to provide access to all the information in his office.

Gilling telephones, Utzon suggests meeting with Hughes away from RAIA, at North Sydney office, rendezvous at Falcon Street Crows Nest.

4.30 p.m. Utzon leaves Bennelong Point office in Wheatland's car for meeting with Hughes in motel room at Shore Motor Inn at Lane Cove arranged by **Mr R.A. Gilling** and returns at 7.30 p.m. Present: Hughes, Humphreys, Walker, Farmer, Buus, Wood, Gilling. Rejects outstanding fee of £51,000 ($102,000) but does agree to advance Utzon £5,000 ($10,000) to pay his staff salaries. Notorious diagram by Hughes showing Utzon's inferior position on the management ladder is drawn. The Shore Motor Inn motel is at Lane Cove on corner of Pacific Hwy & Ryde Road, where the meeting was held.

UTZON STATEMENT TO HUGHES

Utzon writes to Hughes, Minister for PWD:

STATEMENT No. 1:

'I cannot accept the Minister relying on sources such as the RAIA, whose members have never, in spite of several invitations and pressure from me, found it necessary to visit me in my office and study my drawings and the whole case in detail, and therefore all statements from their side have no value.' (p. 1).

'My Consultants, Messers. Ove Arup & Partners, have also endangered the SOH and jeopardised the whole scheme, and you have not given me any possibility to refute Arup's various untruthful and hasty statements.' (p. 2).

'Ove Arup & Partners have ridiculed you as the Minister...' (p. 2).

'If I did not have this attitude to the job, you would not have had the Major and Minor Halls made by Professors Cremer and Gabler and you would not have what we have today — extremely successful acoustical forms of these two halls are, after all, the most important thing in the house.' (p. 3).

STATEMENT No. 2: A SHORT STATEMENT OF MY FINAL ACCOUNTS, WHICH IN DETAIL ARE IN MY OFFICE

'I charge you for what is built and some installation drawings which I know have been carried out by capable people...I also charge for the Stage Technique engineering work of £51,000. No matter if you have another opinion, you have already paid part of the fee to consultants, based on 6% of the engineering component.' (p. 1)

'The drawings which you have not received for Stage 3 I simply refuse to deliver to you for the above–mentioned reasons. This therefore entitles me today to an amount of £615,000 ($1,230,000) which I am sure you are aware I must be paid before you start anybody else who is a member of the same Institute as I am.' (p. 2).

E.H. Farmer taps Utzon on chest with pipe and reassures him they will get on fine. Gilling on CHN 7 TV news at 7 p.m.; Utzon et al return to office 7 p.m. Wheatland talks to Stephen Haag later.

Ashworth talks to Gazzard.

MAR 11   Friday: 9.30 a.m., Hughes telephones Gilling and reads him text of press release.

The Minister requests a reply from Utzon by following Tuesday.

Walter Bunning article. Utzon writes answers in reply for Gazzard to publish on Saturday.

PWD sends Utzon cheque for $10,000 so that he can pay his staff.

Ashworth sees Dr Cobden Parkes.

Staff arrange an exhibition of Utzon's drawings, visited by numerous architects over the afternoon who remain there till 8 p.m.

PWD cheque arrives and is paid into account.

Letter from PWD cannot wait 2 weeks and requires a decision by Tuesday 15th March. Utzon sends a reply.

2.30 p.m. meeting with Nicholl solicitor, leads to meeting with J.M Smythe Q.C. and letter to shake the Government, lasts till 6.30 p.m. Utzon says he was *'quite sure we would be leaving the site but it was quite possible we would return at a later time.'*

4.00 p.m. Special Council Meeting NSW RAIA.

Afternoon: Wheatland removes drawings and sketches from Benelong Point office in boot of car; delivered to Paddington.

MAR 14   Monday: Rally in Town Hall organised by Utzon–in–Charge–Committee.

MAR 15   Tuesday: Negotiations with Hughes are at an end.

Utzon replies to Minister: *'Such a proposal is not only unpractical but quite unacceptable to me.'*

Ashworth receives a message to call on the Minister the following morning.

4.00 p.m.: Ron Gilling is called to Parliament by Hughes and is shown Utzon's reply.

5.30 p.m.: SOHEC meets to discuss the situation.

Prip–Buus rings Colless Tuesday night to tell her Hughes has rejected Utzon's reply and she goes into the office to get copies of letters to distribute to the press.

MARCH 16   Wednesday: Minister writes, *'I have received with deep regret your reply dated 15th March, 1966, ...'* and makes public statement to press saying there would be no difficulty getting reputable architects to work on the project.

9.00 a.m., Ashworth has interview with [Minister of PWD] Hughes.

Utzon's staff pack up office and remove files and personal effects of Utzon.

MAR 17	Thursday: Ashworth and Mr Laurie Thomas (Arts editor of *The Australian* newspaper meet Utzon on the Bennelong Point site to discuss further negotiations — Utzon rejects the idea since he feels there is no chance of compromise being reached at such a late stage.

MAR 17 Thursday: Ashworth and Mr Laurie Thomas (Arts editor of *The Australian* newspaper meet Utzon on the Bennelong Point site to discuss further negotiations — Utzon rejects the idea since he feels there is no chance of compromise being reached at such a late stage.

Farmer, and Crown Solicitor representative come to site and meet Utzon and his solicitor each standing at ends of buildings while solicitors negotiate; Mr Farmer is not permitted to enter Utzon's end of building.

3.00 p.m.: Gilling receives a letter from Hughes saying Utzon has indicated he is unable to continue as Architect.

4.00 p.m.: Special Council Meeting RAIA to consider situation.

MAR 18 Friday: <u>Utzon makes a final claim to 18 March, 1966, for professional services as Architect for sum of $1,595,322.</u>

Legal document setting out temporary rights of two parties does not arrive at 11 a.m., is taken by Nicholl & Nicholl to Crown Solicitor at 9.30 a.m. and is completed at 12.30 p.m. Farmer arrives officially 'taking over' with hordes of newspaper men and spends 35 minutes there. In fact he spent 5 minutes in Utzon's area and did not take over anything; the entire show was a PR exercise; Utzon invites them to stay.

Ryan rings Utzon and expresses surprise at the petition signed by architects working under Hughes in Public Works Department.

Gilling rings asking Utzon to go sailing with him on Sunday 20 March to get close to Utzon but Utzon declines.

Peter B. Hall comes into Government Architect's design office in afternoon and signs 2nd page of petition. Ted Mack is in charge and keeps p. 2.

MAR 19 Saturday: petition signed by 75 of 85 architects in Gov. Arch. Branch is leaked to the press and published on Saturday.

MAR 20 Sunday: Wheatland spends afternoon giving an interview to *Tharunka* UNSW, *Honi Soit* (U Sydney) magazines at Elias Duek–Cohens' flat, Potts Point.

9 p.m. meeting at N. Gruzman house, Double Bay, with Seidler, Epstein, Kollar, Howard, Edmunson, Mackay, Lucas, Duek–Cohen, Rickard — dragged on until late.

MAR 21 Monday: Wheatland busy making application for fiat to prevent work signed by 9 members. Discussion with Clive Evatt at Selbourne Chambers, events later in the day indicate it was a political ploy.

Weatherburn arrives 11.20 a.m. and is sent away. Rudder Littlemore & Rudder ring Mr Weatherburn on Utzon's number! Utzon asks for letter from Ryan for use as an expression of confidence he can take with him to Zürich.

MAR 22   Tuesday: Ashworth and Mr Laurie Thomas have a long interview with Hughes for 2 hours to discuss the entire situation.

Utzon expresses concern about leaving Australia with small amount of money.

MAR 23   Wednesday: Letter from Utzon to Gilling accuses him of failing in his duty as President.

Builder walks off the job leaving the work unfinished on Utzon's Paddington house alterations which were being carried out by Peter Myers.

MAR 24   Thursday: Prip–Buus hands over drawings to Weatherburn, Utzon writes staff references, leaves Bennelong Point at 8 p.m. for meeting on legal advice at Gruzman house lasts till 12.30 a.m.

MAR 25   Friday: London Symphony Orchestra rehearses at SOH site.

Utzon at Bennelong Point office with some staff. He asks Colless to continue working for him and mentions his plans to leave Australia. Prip–Buus and Nayman will leave in April or early May. All the architectural staff finish up.

2.45–5.20 p.m.: Wheatland briefs Ryan, the former Minister on details of affair.

MAR 27   Sunday: Ashworth drives to Palm Beach to speak to Utzon, but Utzon is away. Ashworth telephones later the same day without success and fails to contact Utzon.

MAR 28   Monday: 8 p.m. Meeting in the lower Town Hall of more than 650 members of NSW Chapter

RAIA carries a motion expressing confidence in the actions of Mr R.A. Gilling by 369 to 283 votes. Utzon states his conditions to return. The Chairman refuses to count student member votes which would have changed outcome.

Minister Davis Hughes telephones Ashworth and Mr Laurie Thomas with his final decision — the Government will proceed with its own arrangements.

HTL SOH CONSORTIUM

E.H. Farmer, the Chief Architect of NSW, chairman (b. Perth 6 December 1909), joined GA in 1939, retired as GA at 65 in 1974, D.S. Littlemore, in charge of supervision (b. 1911–d.), Lionel Todd (b. Kingsgrove 27 Feb. 1930–d. 22 Feb. 1998), in charge of documents, Peter Hall, in charge of design (b. 16 May 1931–d. 19 May 1995).

MAR 31   Thursday: Wheatland & Utzon wait till 5.15 p.m. for legal meeting on fee claims at Selbourne Chambers with J.M. Smythe and Nicholls.

| APR 4 | Monday: Shirley Colless starts work at 18 Windsor Street, Paddington, for Utzon. Works till 8.00 p.m. on a massive secret document detailing Utzon's financial claims. There is no telephone connection to the house. |

APR 4 Monday: Shirley Colless starts work at 18 Windsor Street, Paddington, for Utzon. Works till 8.00 p.m. on a massive secret document detailing Utzon's financial claims. There is no telephone connection to the house.

APR 5 Tuesday: Last and highest segment of the tallest roof shell is lowered into position. Colless goes to Utzon house at Palm Beach to type references for Utzon's architectural staff and Elsa Atkins, group certificates.

APR 6 Wednesday: Office picnic at Palm beach, staff collected at the Palm Beach office then drove around to the rocks on east beach side — a marvellous place. Utzon, Lis, Jan, etc attend, afterwards they go to Artransa Studios, French's Forest, for a film, some others went to the Beacon Hill pub.

APR 7 Thursday: Colless working back late prior to the Easter Friday holiday break for Utzon.

APR 18 Monday: Wheatland and Colless drive up in afternoon to Utzon's Palm Beach house which is in uproar while the removalists pack, Jørn, Lis and Jan Utzon, Wheatland, and Colless end day dinning at a local restaurant for dinner.

APR 19 Tuesday: Utzon's replacements are announced: Colless spends the day with Wheatland working hard at 18 Windsor St., Paddington. Wednesday, much running around; Thursday and Friday little happens except clearing things up in office and making arrangements to move drawings out.

APR 24 Jack Zunz and Ove Arup fly to Sydney to see Jørn Utzon who is at Palm Beach, but Utzon refuses to speak to them.

Utzon stays with Wheatland at Hargrave St., Paddington. Shirley Colless works for Utzon from March to immediately prior to his departure.

APR 26 Tuesday evening 7.30 p.m. farewell party for Utzon at the Belvedere Hotel, 81 Bayswater Road, Kings Cross, with Utzon present and attended by Elias Duek–Cohen, Denis Winston, and other members of the *Utzon–in–Charge Committee.*

APR 27 Wednesday: R.A.I.A., NSW Chapter meets and passes a resolution supporting Utzon.

APR 28 Thursday night: Utzon leaves Hargrave Street house where Wheatland's wife Chris is staying, and flies out of Sydney with Lis and children. Bill Wheatland arranges to smuggle them aboard a Qantas flight without the knowledge of the press; Ron Devine sees them off; he breaks the journey for a two week stay in Mexico and visit to the Yucatan before returning to Denmark via New York.

School at Herning; town Centre at Farum (project).

Theatre for Wolfsburg, Germany (competition). 3rd prize.

Farum Town Centre, Denmark: commercial and town plan.

APR Ove Arup writes in Danish to Steen Eiler Rasmussen and to Lis Utzon for a meeting. Lis sends a very unhappy letter in reply.

MAY 5 Thursday: in Sydney, Ove Arup states that collaboration with Utzon began to deteriorate in 1964 about the time Utzon left Denmark. He feels that any halt in work could destroy the Opera House.

11 a.m. Meeting at Hotel Belvedere with acoustic consultant Prof Cremer and ABC represented by Dean Dixon, John Hopkins & Mr Gibb.

MAY 10 Ove Arup in Sydney, talks to media about causes of delay on the Opera House and his frustration with the project.

MAY 17 Crown Solicitor recommends that $160,000 be paid to Utzon without prejudice payment made on 17 May 1966 to release a lien on documents handed over by Utzon's representative. Notes that Utzon's only asset in NSW is his real estate at Bayview.

MAY 18 *SMH* states $150,000 paid to Utzon for Opera House drawings.

MAY 19 Site meeting at which Utzon's drawings for Stage III examined but only 91 can be located.

MAY 24 E.H. Farmer writes to General Manager of the ABC to liaise on requirements with Weatherburn and panel.

MAY 27 ABC 3 hour visit to OH site conducted by Ulmer and Turnbull, meet Mr Weatherburn (the Assistant Government Architect), who is resident there.

JUNE 6 R.W. Askin (NSW Premier) writes to Duckmanton at the ABC promising the co–operation of his Minister for Public Works, Davis Hughes.

First meeting of ABC OH Committee (Operations).

JUNE 7 International Honourary Prize of the Bund Deutscher Architekten (German Architects Association) is presented to Utzon by its Chairman, Conrad Sage at Lubeck, West Germany.

ABC sends a detailed list of its requirements to Haviland and Farmer GA — the first such [external] list.

JUNE 9 Duckmanton presses for a decision on whether the ABC will use the SOH.

JUNE 10 An angry Utzon is quoted as saying, *'Tear it down if you like.'* He asks to have his name removed from the project.

ABC Committee to liaise with Architectural Panel consisting of S. Darling (Supervisor of Buildings Plans) as chairman; Mehaffey (ABC acoustical expert) hold meeting with Weatherburn (AGA), Peter Hall Architect in Charge of Design, and Mr Phil Taylor PWD Mechanical engineer.

JUNE 11 'Opera House' FOUR CORNERS program — PNJ331 by ABC Television.

JUNE 20 Peter Hall leaves on a 12 week three month world study–tour of Europe and USA to research expert thinking on performing arts centres and dual–purpose use auditoria and hires Ben Schlanger from New York to advise, returns in early Oct.

JUNE 24	Midsummer Eve, Friday; Jørn Utzon removes Opera House models from the Hellebæk Factory and burns them on the beach at Stranvej, Ålsgård.
JULY 4	Peter Hall scheduled to have first conference with Ove Arup and Dr Jordan in London. Plans for Peter Hall to meet Mr Mehaffey from ABC there.
AUG	The State Office Building, designed by Ken Woolley, on Macquarie, Phillip and Bent Streets, is finally occupied after 3½ years. It was designed and supervised by PWD and demonstrated a serious failure to manage such a large project effectively. The Contract was signed on 24 Dec. 1962 with Perini Australia Pty Ltd for $11,523,532 and it was completed for $15,586,725 — an increase of 35%.
AUG 21	Utzon sells parcel of land owned in fee simple at Bayview (Vol. 9237, Fol. 138) to Beacon Investments P/L, Manly (N.R. Smart & T.S. Keen) for $13,000. Also included as a separate transaction, Utzon sells a further parcel Lot 2, D.P. 224856 (whole, Vol. 10176, Fol. 101) for $70,000 to Beacon Investments P/L, Manly. Total amount realised from the sale is $83,000.
AUG 25	Thursday. Address in Reply by Ryan (41st Parliament–3rd Session, see *Hansard* No. 9, pp. 583–588). The Opposition attacks Hughes over Utzon's withdrawal, the lack of genuine progress, and failure of the Minister to take decisions. Hughes defends his actions in Utzon's resignation, stating it was by Utzon's own decision and responds: *'The withdrawal of Mr. Utzon was certainly not sought, desired or expected but the approach of the new [HTL] panel has brought new life and a new spirit to the project.'* Former Minister Ryan replies: *'All you have done is to knock up a few more seats, provide a few less rooms, and put in a few extra toilets'* and adds, *'the way in which he [Hughes] implemented this ministerial control was unprecedented.'* Ryan comments: *'The Minister decided very obviously that some scapegoat had to be found to justify the earlier political criticism. Though he made frantic efforts to unearth an alleged scandal that would nail the previous administration he failed to do so.'* He defends Utzon's performance, saying, *'The escalation in the cost of the opera house had very little to do with the architect.'*
AUG 26	Askin replies, *'We inherited an absolute shemozzle from a succession of Labor Governments.'*
SEPT	Alex C. Popov (b. Shanghai 1942–) arrives in London on his way to Copenhagen, visits Richard Neville in Holland Park. Lives in London until 1969, sharing a house with Neil Burley and Michael Kitching, artist (1968–70).
SEPT 1	Thursday. *Sydney Opera House (Amendment) Bill* debate (41st Parliament–3rd Session, see *Hansard* No. 12, pp. 734–743). Ryan calls for a debate on the withdrawal of Utzon.
SEPT 15	Duckmanton still has not had a chance to speak to D. Hughes about ABC requirements at SOH; Mehaffey has discussions with Prof. L Cremer.

SEPT 16 The new Metropolitan Opera House by Wallace Harrison is inaugurated with the world premier of Samuel Barber's *Antony and Cleopatra*, produced by Zeffirelli. Designed by Wallace Harrison, with a traditional horseshoe auditorium and 4 balconies and capacity of 3,824 (253 standing), it was completed last after the Philharmonic Hall (1962) by Max Abramovitz, and the New York State Theatre (1964) by Philip Johnson. The overall plan of the Lincoln Centre for the Performing Arts (1962–68) was by Harrison & Abramovitz. Although Harrison was assisted by some talented collaborating architects who created some good interiors, the urban space outside is far from lively.

SEPT 28 Wednesday: 2nd reading *Sydney Opera House (Amendment) Bill* (41st Parliament–3rd Session, see *Hansard*, No. 20, pp. 1284–1315). Hughes justifies his action in taking over control of the Opera House project: 'It is in this area where proper planning and preparation of working drawings and documents, proper control over cost, and total programming, I repeat, total programming, became possible so far as the present Government is concerned.'

SEPT 29 Thursday. 2nd reading *Sydney Opera House (Amendment) Bill* (see *Hansard*, No. 21, pp. 1356–1387).

SEPT Peter Hall is expected back from overseas at the end of September.

OCT 6 Thursday. *Sydney Opera House (Amendment) Bill*, 2nd reading (41st Parliament–3rd Session, see *Hansard* No. 24, pp. 1579–1606).

OCT 11 Tuesday. *Sydney Opera House (Amendment) Bill* 2nd reading (see *Hansard* No. 25, 41st Parliament–3rd Session, pp. 1645–1655).

OCT *Sydney Opera House (Amendment) Act* authorises expenditure up to $37.5 million. It was impossibly low at $11.9 million less than the August 30, 1965, estimate.

NOV 11 Peter Hall returns to Sydney in time for a meeting with *ABC Operations Committee*.

NOV 24 T.S. Duckmanton meets the NSW Minister for Public Works to discuss latest developments of SOH design.

DEC Public debate about the role and size of Major and Minor halls; Elizabethan Theatre Trust battles the ABC.

Ben Schlanger, an architect specialising in interior design from New York, and T.E. Bean (former Gen. Manager of Royal Festival Hall) are brought to Sydney. Schlanger advises on how to increase seating in the halls and Bean advises on the possible uses of areas within the Opera House.

DEC 8 D. Hughes asks **Dr Coombes** (Elizabethan Theatre Trust) and **T.S. Duckmanton** (ABC) to join a committee with Mr Haviland to advise the Minister and his officers, the aim being to by–pass and supplant the existing SOH Trust, thereby avoiding criticism which would be caused by disbanding it or forcing its members to resign. Both men wisely reject his invitation and Hughes' tactic fails.

DEC 12 Hall, Todd & Littlemore panel submit *Review of Programme* report which concludes a dual–purpose hall is unworkable. They recommend instead that the Major Hall should be a single–purpose concert hall and opera be transferred to the Minor Hall, on the grounds that the multi–purpose hall would not be functionally satisfactory. The alternative convertible hall type was not touched upon in the report.

DEC 21   Dr H.C. (Nugget) Coombes, founder and chairman of the Australian Elizabethan Theatre Trust, writes to D. Hughes to press the claims of opera in the major auditorium.

1966   Utzon travels in the United States, Switzerland and Denmark.

1967

JAN 17   Crews at Bennelong Point lower the 2,194th or last precast segment of the roof into place (last crownpiece on A4).

JAN 23   Coombs writes to ABC with suggestions for keeping the Major Hall as a dual–purpose auditorium, and again on Jan 31; the ABC rejects his proposals on both occasions.

FEB   Stage II is completed for $13,165,955.

FEB 13   D. Hughes is elected to The Council of the Univ. of New England.

FEB 16   Opera House Trust backs the Elizabethan Theatre Trust in opposing changes and the retention of a dual–purpose auditorium.

FEB 20   Opera House Trust sends letter to D. Hughes attacking the recommendations of the HTL Architectural Panel and the ABC. Neil Hutchison (ABC) resigns from the OHT over this issue and George Molnar writes a persuasive article in favour of Utzon's original concept.

FEB 27   Utzon in *The Australian* states he now knows how to design the Major Hall to satisfy the ABC and ETT requirements and is willing to submit to the stringent conditions that Davis Hughes laid down the previous year. Askin rejects the offer as 'impractical.'

FEB 28   Utzon indicates his willingness to return and appeals to minister 'Let me finish the job' and agrees to strict controls. Stage III contract is awarded for paving and cladding, but the material is not not what Utzon selected.

MAR   5,000 copies of **E. Duek–Cohen** (ed.), *utzon and the sydney opera house*, are published with text written by **Donald Horne** (pp. 5–40) using material prepared by Bill Wheatland to defend Utzon. In October 1998, the unsold copies were reissued with a new Foreword and Addendum to update the account. It came too late.

MAR 21   Hughes announces there will be no opera facilities in Major Hall, which now becomes a single purpose concert hall. Minor Hall is changed from drama theatre to opera theatre. It is decided that the Major Hall is to be designed as a single purpose concert hall seating 2,800 and R.T. close to 2 seconds. This results in a 'downgrading' of opera and drama to permit a single–purpose concert hall: opera to the Minor

Hall, Drama to Experimental Theatre, Experimental Theatre to Rehearsal Room, and so forth. These to be used for purposes other than originally intended, numerous alterations to the fabric will be necessary to accomplish this, etc.

MAR 31 Utzon staying at Suite 1522, Ala Moana Building, Honolulu, Hawaii until the beginning of May close by Peer Abben's office.

MAR 27 Opera House to be called Arts Centre — Hughes announces that Main Hall is to be used for concerts only.

MAY Yuzo Mikami completes his confidential report for Ove Arup & Partners, commissioned as a precaution in the event the engineering consultant is asked to take over the work: *DRAFT REPORT ON MAJOR HALL AUDITORIUM DESIGN, SYDNEY OPERA HOUSE,* London, May 1967.

> **MIKAMI MAJOR HALL AUDITORIUM DESIGN REPORT**
> Mikami investigates acoustic feasibility of multi–purpose and convertible hall approaches, rejects former but considers that convertible hall will produce an acceptable result. Pt. IV Conclusion: '..the recent decision made on the use of the Major Hall was based on insufficient and one–sided technical information which had to be produced hastily and, therefore, was erroneous. The consequence of the decision will not only result in chaotic and damaging alterations inside the building as already mentioned but also will have a seriously damaging effect on the architectural value of the building.' p. 13.

JUNE 30 *Auditor General Report, 1966–67*: C.17, Official visit abroad by D. Hughes' Treasury advance.

JULY 15 D. Hughes away on trip to Japan.

NOV 2 Deputy Commissioner of Taxation issues Notice under Section 218 to Jørn Oberg Utzon, 19 Alexander Crescent, BAYVIEW, for tax owing to the amount $91,310.70

DEC 5 Nicholl & Nicholl, 9 Bligh Street, SYDNEY, issue Writ No. 8754 of 1967 on Utzon's behalf as plaintiff against Minister for Public Works for fees owing.

DEC 12 ABC Documentary 'Utzon' directed by Peter Luck goes to air. Luck earlier interviewed Utzon on the island of Styrso, Sweden, opposite Naset where he was holidaying. Styrso is approximately 8 km off the west coast and 16 km southwest from Göteborg.

1968

Sketch of Bagsværd Church is presented and unanimously accepted by the parochial council. Client is Bagsværd parochial church council and its representative **The Reverend, Dean Svend Simonsen**.

Utsep Mobler Flexible Furniture (project)

FEB 19 Public Meeting in the Sydney Town Hall at 1.00–2.00 p.m. convened by Mrs Elizabeth Price, Chaired by the Rev. A.P.B. Bennie, Warden of St Paul's College, University of Sydney, speakers included P.N. Ryan, Roger Covell, Elias Duek–Cohen. Utzon sends a short tape recorded message expressing his willingness to return. The issue of his participation is presented in the news media.

MAR 14 Utzon's tax debt to Commonwealth is reduced to $80,130.95 by payment of $11,179.75.

MAY 24 Amount tax owing is reduced to $57,835.45 by payment of a further $22,295.50 to Tax Office.

JULY 27 Estimates that Sydney Opera House costs will soar to between $100m and $120m reported to be made by Peter Hall causes acute embarrassment in the Hughes camp after getting rid of Utzon and the Minister's promise to control costs and to end indefinite delays.

SEPT 4 Hall Todd & Littlemore later advise Davis Hughes of their estimate of $85 million to complete the new Opera House and promise it can be completed by the end of 1972. Hughes announces this to public, becomes Deputy Leader of the Country Party in NSW.

SEPT 13 Applied Science Building, University of NSW, opened. Ove Arup & Partners appointed structural consultants in 1965 by Cobden Parkes, Univ. Arch. because OA & P were in financial difficulties following the building slump after Sep. 1965.

Death of Sigfried Giedion in Munich, Germany.

GIEDION

Sigfried Giedion, b. Switzerland 1894, and studied art history in Zurich, Berlin, dies at Munich in 1968 aged 74. At Weimar he was associated with Walter Gropius, with whom he played an important part in the introduction of modern architecture in Switzerland. He revised the 5th edition of *Space Time and Architecture*, to include a new chapter on Utzon in September 1966 while staying at the American Academy, Rome. In September 1966, Giedion wrote: 'In his own personality Utzon mirrors our period in all its complexity. In architecture Utzon stands for the right of expression as the supreme law, as it has always been supreme for all creative artists.'

JULY   The Sydney Opera House Society is launched 'to encourage the completion of the Opera House to the highest standard…' with Gordon Jacob Samuels as its first President. The society was active till 1978. Peter Scriven, the puppeteer, was the convenor.

1969

 School Centre with Technical College, Herning, Denmark (project).

 Espansiva Byg A/S Timber Component House System (project).

Jeddah Sports Layout and stadium for National Sports Centre, Saudi Arabia (project).

DEC   National Museum for study of landscape at Hammershus on Bornholm. Competition requires visitor centre, restaurant and cafeteria, car parking. Jørn Utzon is disgusted and does not bother to pick up drawings.

Utzon completes his plans for the Zürich Theatre in 1969; after making many adjustments for the traffic requirements and taking into account new requirements to satisfy a series of theatre directors. The 1970 cost estimate was calculated by Utzon's Swiss partners.

MAR 18   **Charles Cutler** (Orange) Deputy Premier presents *Sydney Opera House (Amendment) Bill*, 7.39 p.m., 18 March, 1969, which sets a maximum age of 70 for membership if the SOH Trust and authorises the total expenditure of $85,000,000 with no provision for the 10 per cent margin usually provided in such legislation. This amount includes the $32,000,000 already expended to that date and represents an increase of $35,000,000 in the estimate in the 3 years since Utzon departed.

MAR 19   Second reading debate on bill, P.N. Ryan (former Labor Minister for Public Works), as Opposition spokesman, refers to the stage installation (machinery) which cost $600 to $800 a tone to erect, now sold for $20 ton as scrap. The new amount allowed for stage machinery is revealed to be $6,700,000 compared to the original contract of $4,300,000. The review of programme results in a surplus of $1 million.

Ryan says: '*I believe the sacking of Utzon was the greatest tragedy that happened in the history of the Opera House…His resignation was a loss to this country. It was also a tragedy. Now we must face not $50,000,000 but $85,000,000 as the final cost, but it is likely to go even higher. I predict now that this building will not be finished for $85,000,000.*' (*Hansard*, p. 4778).

Ryan further declares Utzon has submitted drawings to him of the Major Hall for a multi–purpose hall suitable for both concert and opera, with seating for 2,800 resulting from further collaboration with Dr. Cremer and Dr. Gabler in Berlin. Ryan calls on the Government not to proceed with the bill but to appoint an all–party committee to examine alternatives saying: '*We know that, from the outside, this building is an architectural masterpiece. The building will be false if the present plans are implemented. It will be architecturally false: it will not be the building it should have been.'* (p. 4642). The Bill is passed.

APR 10 Writ No. 8754 served on Minister for Public Works 4.30 p.m., from Robert Warren Nicholl on behalf of Jørn Utzon for the sum of $349,342.20. Represented by Counsel Mr. P.M. Woodward Q.C.

APR 11 Utzon writes to Stadtbaumeister, Zürich, that he has been working hard on theatre project to meet requirements, and has a serious financial loss on the project on account of the many different designs he has submitted in order to meet the changing requirements. Refers to crucial vote to decide future of the project.

MAY 31 Lin Oberg Utzon marries **Alexander Popov** (b. 3 February 1942) son of Constantin Popov and Zenaida Popov. He studied at Royal Academy with standing 1969–1972 for 3½ years. In 1970 Popov won National Bank Student Scholarship for 1 year project on gas stations. Lin is 23, Popov 27.

JULY 21 **At 02:56 GMT Neil Alden Armstrong, command pilot of the Apoloo 11 mission, sets foot on the moon, on the Sea of Tranquility**

AUG 12 Labor Opposition attacks Government travel rorts: in recent past: Premier, Treasurer have gone on world tour, as have Ministers for Public Works [D. Hughes — 1 world tour, 2 to Japan], Local Government, Transport. In past 4 years, since May 1965, 11 Ministers have had 18 overseas trips, 7 world tours, 4 visited Japan. (J.J. Maloney, Hansard, vol. 80, p. 101)

1970

Utzon is awarded the Mobel Prize for furniture design for his 8108 chair.

JAN Nicholl & Nicholl solicitors writ No. 8754 of 1967, against Minister PWD for $349,342 of Utzon's fees still outstanding. The plaintiff was paid $1,250,000 for his services of a total due him of $1,599,342.20.

FEB 10 Proposed settlement of PWD fees to pay $180,000, Utzon represented by Bannon Q.C.

MAR Cost control problems begin to appear; HTL unable to reach any unified or firm conclusions on cost control measures.

MAY **Vietnam Moratorium marches in Australian cities.**

A.L. Bacon, General Manager (Feb 1968–Nov 1971), announces that Opera House will open in March 1973.

JUNE 23 Government agrees to pay Utzon $46,000 in outstanding fees.

AUG 25 Tuesday: Utzon is absent from his Hellebæk home in Sweden.

SEPT **Second series of Moratorium marches.**

OCT 23   Criticism of overseas visits by members of Cabinet — Estimate item for overseas travel expenses $16,000, comment by Mason. (*Hansard*, vol 62, p. 1,867).

NOV 18   Death of **Aage Utzon**, Jørn's father. Obituary in *Sejl og Motor* (Sail and Motor) Jan 1971, p. 26. He is buried in Hellebæk churchyard with a large flat stone bearing just the name UTZON carved in capital letters.

1971–79   **The Kuwait National Assembly Complex**, Kuwait City, Kuwait.Construction 1979–83. J. Utzon architect, M. Walt structural engineer, J.B. Oveseu mechanical engineer. Designed in 1971, altered scheme done in November 1973

1971–72;   Visiting Professor, University of Hawaii, Manoa, design studio class and course in climatology. Present in
1973   Hawaii during Fall and Spring Semesters September 1971–72 & 1973 academic years. (1971–72; 1973).

1971–72   **'Can Lis', Jørn Utzon House**, sandstone house with courts in a pine grove on the cliff edge, on Cala media luna, Colonia del Silencio, south of Porto Petro, by way of Santanyi, on the southeast coast of Mallorca. Similarities with the 4th and 5th schemes for Utzon's Kara Crescent, Bayview, house designed in Australia.

1971

Jørn & Lis Utzon move to Mallorca permanently.

Davis Hughes visits England with wife Phillipa, cancels Jack Zunz's booking of Royal Shakespeare Company's celebrated production of *Much Ado About Nothing*, by Ronald Ayre, and insists on *Fiddler on the Roof*.

MAR   **Prime Minister William McMahon announces gradual withdrawal of 1,000 personnel from South Vietnam.**

MAR 24   **Ane Jacobsen** (b Copenhagen 11 Feb 1902) dies in Copenhagen. Jacobsen criticised the joinery of Utzon's Fredensborg project.

APR   **Largest US anti–war march draws 500,000 demonstrators to Washington.**

MAY 13   Confidential minute expresses growing concern that end of 1972 is unrealistic date of completion. Fears are now expressed that the $85 million budget figure will be exceeded by $5 to 10 million.

MAY 27   Heated Cost Control Meeting between HTL panel and quantity surveyors at which Todd complains at the lack of effective cost controls.

JUNE 15   Utzon makes a radical design for a 10.5 m long aluminium hull yacht built by Al–Boats, Helsingør, for family sailing. Its hull is a siamese twin form splitting at the back into two sterns leading it to be described as a tripple–ender 'tre–delingen af haekken' reminiscent of a catamaran. The boat has a displacement of 4 tons, beam of 3.05 m and draught of 1.85 m and carried a sail of 50 m² with diesel motor.

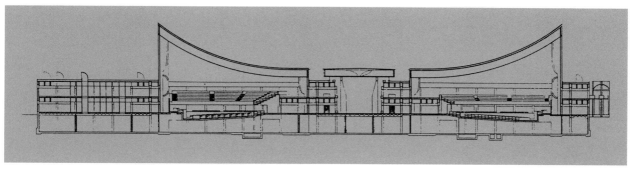

The Kuwait National Assembly Complex, Kuwait City, section

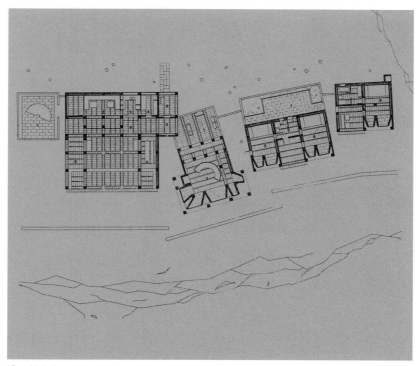

'Can Lis', Jørn Utzon House, plan of pavillion units.

1971   Zürich: growing public opposition to the traffic proposals in Zürich forces the cancellation of the Theatre project. In 1972 the Federal Swiss Government orders a temporary halt to all public buildings — federal, cantonal and communal — as a way of curbing inflation.

SEPT 21   It is announced that Utzon will lecture in design at U of Hawaii.

OCT 5   Hughes seeks Cabinet approval to exceed the 4 September 1968 estimate of $85 million which was approved by Parliament on 18 March 1969 as part of its budget.

1972

     Parliament and Congress Centre, Kuwait, 1st prize.

MAR   Final cost of SOH calculated at $102 million.

JUNE   **Mr Stanley Haviland** (b. 1909–72) dies aged 73. He was Under–Secretary of the Department of Local Government before his appointment as Chairman of the SOH Committee.

AUG   **Last US ground combat troops withdrawn from South Vietnam.**

NOV 15   Davis Hughes makes his last speech to the NSW Parliament, concluding: "When Her Majesty comes here on 20th October next year [1973], everybody here in Australia will be proud of the opera house.' (*Hansard*, s.3, vol.102, p. 2749).

NOV 25   4 acres of land at Kora Crescent, Bayview, previously owned by Utzon, are sold by the new owner Alderman Griffin through Richardson & Walsh for $175,000.

DEC 5   **Edward Gough Whitlam is elected Prime Minister of Australia heading the first Labor government in Canberra since Benedict Chifley in 1949.**

DEC   **Gough Whitlam orders last Australian troops withdrawal, conscription and military service is abandoned.**

1973

     Gold Medal, RAIA, awarded in Australia to Utzon

JAN 17   Sir Davis Hughes resigns from the NSW Parliament and as Minister for Public Works to take up post as NSW Agent–General in London. In by–election that follows, on 17 Feb. 1973, David Leach is elected to replace Hughes. After a Cabinet reshuffle the Hon. Leon Ashton Punch (Wentworthville) is appointed Minister for Public Works in his place.

Small sports palace, dome, 1960. Pier luigi Nervi

FEB 17   By–elections in Armidale, Hawkesbury, Byron.

MAR 15   Stuart Bacon, the first General Manager of SOH, resigns and is succeeded by Frank Barnes, 1973–79.

APR   Construction begins on Bagsværd Church.

APR 30   Utzon in Honolulu, Hawaii, is interviewed by *Women's Day* reporter Susan Dunlop earlier that month. Still there on 24 September.

JUNE   Stage III completed for $80,383,130.

SEPT 24   Contacted in Hawaii, Utzon is working on Kuwait project twice size of Opera House. This is his second visit lecturing at University of Hawaii, School of Architecture.

OCT 6   **Yom Kippur war between Israel, Syria, and Egypt, cease fire declared Oct 24.OPEC restricts supply of oil and quadruples price of oil exports.**

OCT 20   **Official opening of SOH by Queen Elizabeth II.** Final cost given as $98,709,085 (does not include cost of organ)..

Officially launched at 3.30 p.m. when four tugs pull 16 pink ribbons from the peaks of the white roof shells; 45 knot winds made celebration difficult; 2000 yachts and small boats, 15,000 spectators on the site and estimated 3 million television viewers around the world. Flypast of nine RAAF FIII bombers, 60,000 multi–coloured balloons released.

According to Jan Utzon, Jørn Utzon is on a two week touring holiday in Spain. He had recently left the University of Hawaii, where he was teaching part–time, to return to Denmark by way of South–East Asia.

NOV 17   State Election. The Askin government is returned.

1974

Danish Government prohibits all building work in the aftermath of ARAB–ISRAELI WAR and oil hike. Bagsværd is temporarily halted.

MAY   Minister for Public Works announces that the final bill for SOH is $102 million. All but $A9,300,000 was raised by lotteries; this outstanding amount was borrowed from State Treasury as bridging finance, to be repaid over 12 months from further lotteries.

1975

APR 30   Saigon falls.

FIRST PERFORMANCES

CONCERT HALL

1972 DEC 17   1st test concert given by SSO, conducted by Bernard Heinze.

1973 JAN 21   2nd test in morning.

1973 APR 10   1st recital in the complex by pianist Renola Costantino.

1973 JUL 19   Gala World Premier of the Australian ballet's film *Don Quixote*

1973 SEP 29   1st public performance by SSO conducted by Charles Mackerras with soloist Birgit Nilsson.

OPERA THEATRE

1973 JAN 21   1st test program on afternoon.

1973 JUL 28   1st test opera presented was the Australian opera, *Fall of the House of Usher*, by Larry Sitsky and Dalgerie, by James Penberthy.

1973 SEP 28   1st public performance by the Australian Opera Company of *War and Peace* by Sergei Prokofiev.

MUSIC ROOM

1972 OCT 1   1st concert given by Fidelio String Quartet, Lauris Elms and Donald Westlake.

1973 OCT 2   1st public performance by Musica Viva Australia of Carl Pini Quartet.

DRAMA THEATRE

1972 AUG 28   1st test performance, a program of Australian poems called *The Australian Dream*.

1973 OCT 1   1st public performance of Shakespeare's *Richard II* by the Old Tote Theatre Company.

CONDUCTED TOURS

1973 JUL 1   1st conducted tours of the Opera House as an almost finished structure.

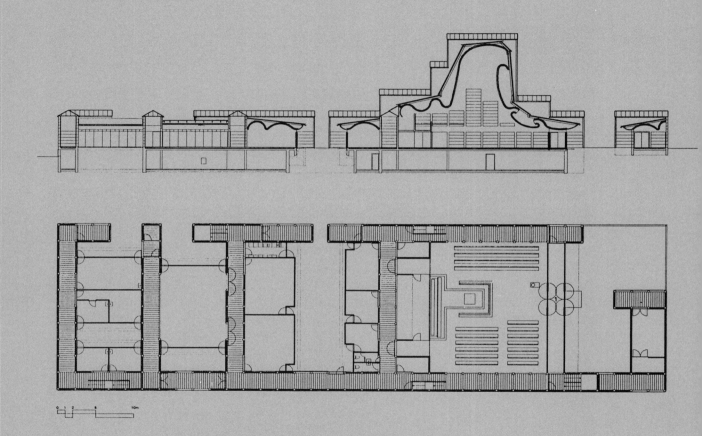

Bagsværd Church at Bagsværd Hovegade, section and floor plan

1976

MAR 8   Sir Ove Arup interview on function and aesthetic in *Politiken*.

MAY 11   **Alvar Aalto** (b near Jyvaskyla 3 Feb 1898) dies in Helsinki. Aalto had been the leading Scandinavian architect and modernist, much admired by Utzon.

MAY 31   Architect's Final Certificate issued to Principal 31 May by which time the cost of SOH has increased to about $100.8 million, not including the carpark, the organ (still being built) or the enlargement of the orchestra pit in the Opera Theatre, which was carried out subsequently. Costs: STAGE I, $5,390,681; STAGE II, $12,897,717; STAGE III, c.$82,500,000; TOTAL, $100,788,398.

AUG 15   Bagsværd Church at Bagsværd Hovegade 189–91, Copenhagen, inaugurated. Lin Utzon collaborates successfully with her father to produce all the textiles for Bagsværd.

AUG 29   **The Amir of Kuwait suspends four articles of the Constitution dealing with the National Assembly, the Majlis–al–Umma.**

1978

MAY   Utzon and Lis are in Honolulu, Hawaii.

JUNE 19   Utzon Exhibition at RIBA HQ Portland Place, London, June 19–30.

JUNE 20   Royal Institute of British Architects' Gold Medal awarded 8.15 p.m., sponsored by Sir Denys Lasdun. Reply from Norman Foster. For text of address by Lasdun see *RIBA Journal,* Oct. 1978, vol. 85, no. 10, p.425–27. Utzon is introduced as Professor of Architecture at Hawaii University.

1978   Zürich Schauspielhaus (b. 1888–89, *Haus zum Pfauen* or House of the Peacock), following the decision not to proceed with Utzon's new theatre in 1976–78, is completely remodelled.

JULY   Construction of the Kuwait National Assembly starts.

1979

             Lakerol Prize is awarded to Utzon.

MAY   SOH organ completed at cost of $1,200,000; original cost estimated at $400,000.

JUNE   Søpavillon by Vilhelm Dahlerup on Lake Peblinge, 1894, plan to replace it by indoor Swimming Hall, Copenhagen, baths and restaurant dropped, the original building is restored instead.

             Transformations in Modern Architecture exhibition by Arthur Drexler, MOMA, New York, p. 29.

⌂ **SEPT**   Foreningens project for heart education centre planned for Skagen, Jutland, for 200 people to cost 30 million kr. Bent Wellejus, administrator, and Prof. A. Tybjaerg Hansen. Jan + Jørn Utzon.

1980

     Jan Utzon completes a timber house for his family and wife Barbara situated in farmland outside Esrum, based on the 1969 Espansiva principle, costing Kr 250,000.

≈   Can Lin House, added near Utzon's 1970 Can Lis House, on Mallorca, designed by son–in–law, Alex Popov.

MAY   Utzon staying in Denmark at Hellebæk house.

AUG 24   Amir of Kuwait issues decree establishing an elected legislature before the end of February 1981.

1981

FEB   Utzon staying in Hawaii.

FEB 23   A new Majlis is elected in Kuwait.

◐ **NOV 23**   Utzon is awarded the Danske Arkitekters Landsforbund prize and Kr 75,000 from Søren Nielsen.

DEC   Lin Utzon and her family visit Sydney and are shown around SOH by Ava Hubble, then return to Denmark early in 1982.

1982

MAY 28   Utzon staying in Spain on holidays.

FEB 3   Wednesday morning: **Dr Wilhelm Lassen Jordan** dies aged 72.

JORDAN

Wilhelm Jordan (b. 1910), from Rosskilde DK, is carried out by a strong rip and is pulled from the surf at the pipeline Manly between North and South Steyne beaches. He came to Sydney as the guest of the PWD and had a meeting with the Opera Company the previous day about electronic amplification in the Minor Hall; this was later denied. He was survived by his young wife Ebba, who died 3 months later on her return to Denmark. Jordan was endorsed as the Acoustical Consultant to the SOH in Nov. 1957. He achieved recognition for his work on Radiohus in Copenhagen and was the author of *Acoustical design of Concert Halls and Theatres* (1980).

⊡	**AUTUMN**	Lin Utzon returns to Sydney for an exhibition of her porcelain designs which are shown in several cities.
◯	**AUG**	Alvar Aalto Medal, Helsinki, Finland.

1983

⊡	**JUNE**	An exhibition of Utzon's designs for the Opera House forecourt and pedestrian and vehicular approaches is mounted at the SOH by the RAIA.
	OCT 16	Neville Wran invites Utzon back on the CHN 9 *Sunday* programme to rebuild the SOH interiors; it is a political stunt to divert media attention; no proper government approach is made to Utzon and the initiative lapses.
	NOV 3	Utzon travels in Spain.
	DEC	Kuwait National Assembly 90% complete. Opens in 1984 at cost of 25,869,703 Kuwait dinars ($4,296 million).

1984

	APR 23	**Jan Utzon** visits Australia to design a holiday resort at Wild Duck Island, 145 km north of Rockhampton, Qld., with Mr Desmond Muirhead and promoter, Sir Francis Hasset. Utzon is ill at the time.

1985

	JAN 13	**Lin Utzon's** Royal Copenhagen Porcelain bowls and vases in the Patina series are decorated with a deep cobalt–blue in–glaze decoration, contrasting with an application of matt platinum over the glaze.
	FEB 20	Fresh legislative elections to the Majlis National Assembly.
⊡	**SEPT**	Hotel and Congress Centre on Langelinie, Copenhagen; project for Kr 125 M. is jointly proposed by Jørn Utzon with entrepreneur H.Hoffmann & Sonner A/S.

1986

		Leif Kristensen completes first accommodation review of Sydney Opera House.
	FEB 16	Niels–Prize (commemorating Niels Matthiasen) is awarded to Utzon of DK 100,000 kroner.
	JULY	The Kuwait Majlis is dissolved by Amiri decree

SEPT 25   Last Opera House Lottery drawn: more than 86.7 million tickets were sold (1957–86) and the $102m cost of the Opera House was paid by 1976; total revenue raised was A$502.3m with total payouts of A$327.726m leaving $174.574million. Prize winners: Grahame Thorne was kidnapped (later murdered) in July 1960 after his parents won $100,000; actor Robert Levis (1965); last winner Mr Antoni Krzton.

SEPT   Paustian furniture showroom, 2,000 m², Copenhagen, by Utzon Associates with his sons Jan and Kim is completed in May 1987; H.Hoffmann & Sonner A/S acted as entrepreneur for Paustian A/S.

1987

FEB 18   Further discussion of Utzon's Hotel and Congress Centre proposal at Langelinie takes place.

MAY   Paustian Furniture Showroom Centre is completed and, later, is awarded the Betonelement – Prisen.

1987   Lin Utzon creates scenography and lighting for Warren Spear's, 'Rowing in Eden', a ballet performed by the Royal Danish Ballet.

OCT 19   **Wall Street, N.Y.: in the first hour of trading the Dow Jones index plunges 104 points, losing 4.6% of its value. In the next half hour it falls a further 104 points. In just one day, the Dow falls 22.6%, the largest stock market crash in history, dwarfing the 11.6% fall on Black Tuesday in 1929.**

1988

The Fritz Schumacher Prize is awarded to Utzon.

Leif Kristensen completes second accommodation review of the Sydney Opera House. Out of this process came later proposals for museum and exhibition spaces

Prior to the implementation of the upgrade programme, the State Government spent $34.6 million on refurbishing the forecourt and construction of the concourse and arcade, supervised by Andrew Anderson (Government Architect) and Les Reedman (Assistant GA). The project was approved by Neville Wran, NSW Premier.

FEB 5   **Ove Nyquist Arup** dies aged 93

APR 7   Danish Museum for Modern Art, Fredensborg, 3,000 m² project, by Jørn with Jan & Kim Utzon for client Erik & Margit Brandt.

APR 9   Thomas Molvig curates Jørn Utzon exhibition by 14 students at Århus Architecture School, Nørreport 20, Århus. It is later sent to the Pompidou Centre, Paris, as the official exhibition representing Denmark. Steen Eiler Rasmussen provided support as visiting professor.

APR 10	Jørn Utzon gives lectures and studios at Århus architecture school at Nørreport 20.
APR 27	Utzon and Chr. Islef make proposal for 1.5 billion kr. redevelopment of south basin of Kalkbrænderi from Svanemollen power station around to Paustian Centre discussed with Mayor Egon Weidekamp, in collaboration with Jan + Kim.
JUNE 3	*The Building of the Century exhibition*, curated by Paul Bentley, opens in the Exhibition Hall at the SOH. Closes 31 March 1989. For review see 'The Harbour Swan,' *Time Australia*, v. 3, no. 29, July 18, 1988, p. 60–64.
JUNE 28	Hotel at Kalundborg, west Zealand, Denmark, project by Jørn Utzon.
JULY	Bornholm (2 projects): Naturama science museum project at Gudhjim; history museum with shops and restaurant at Hammerhavn.

NICHOLAS FRANK GREINER
(b. 1947–), Premier/Treasurer/Minister of Ethnic and Aboriginal Affairs 1988–92, commissions the NSW Public Works Department to carry out an upgrade program (UG1) after 15 years of neglect, 'to restore the building to top condition,' and to establish a system of asset management which would, 'ensure the survival of the house for future generations.' For the first five years work includes repair to structures supporting the broadwalk, conservation of Concert Hall ceiling surfaces, upgrading of services and excavation of a works site office below the podium, joints between the tile lids (1,056,000 tiles) on the roof were waterproofed with sealant, etc. (*SOHUP*, *Progress Report*, 1993). The 1994 cost estimate of $113 million increased to $120 million by 1997.

1989

	Mr Peter Collins, the NSW Minister for the Arts, announces that State Government funds are to be spread over a 10–year period on 652 identifiable SOH projects requiring attention.
MAR 2	Leif Kristensen submits proposals and drawings for a museum and cafe in the gardens, adjacent to the Man O' War steps to house a permanent exhibition on the history, design and construction of the House. Also completes schemes for improvements to Playhouse stage/backstage and convention centre.
APR	Rehearsal Hall (renamed the Broadwalk Studio in 1986) closed as a temporary measure to facilitate construction below Exhibition Hall/Library space and provide temporary accommodation for Public Works Department. In addition, the Broadwalk Studio did not comply with new fire regulations and required heavy subsidization in a time of acute budgetary pressures.

OCT   Orchard Hall, Shibuya (Tokyo) is completed by Yuzo Mikami with a dual purpose convertible hall. The stage enclosure retracts into backstage mechanically in three parts to provide reverberation times of 2.0 seconds and 1.6 seconds. Changeover takes less than 24 hrs. it has 2,150 seats for concerts, 1,928 seats for opera.

1990

               Lin Utzon creates scenography and lighting for director, Warren Spear's, dance performance of Skagen' for New Danish Dance Theatre.

FEB 14   Controversial project for 155m skyscraper on hill top at Århus and boutique complex to cost Kr. 700 million, provides 36,000 m² space. It is rejected as unsuitable. The site is opposite the State Library, Århus University on Randesvej and Nørrebrogade and dominates the city.

JUNE 30   In addition to the funds spent as part of the Government's UG1 Programme, in 1989–90, the Opera House Trust spends $10 million on major maintenance.

AUG 2   **Iraqi troops invade Kuwait; Baghdad announces overthrow of the Kuwait government.**

1991

JAN 17   Operation Desert Storm begins with allied bombing of strategic targets in Baghdad.

FEB 24   Allies launch ground offensive noon Sydney time.

FEB 27   **Tuesday morning, the first Kuwaiti soldiers enter Kuwait city. Baghdad says its withdrawal from Kuwait is complete. Parliament building is set on fire before Republican Guard leaves city.**

JULY   Restoration and rebuilding of the National Assembly, Kuwait, commences by joint effort of the Emergency and Reconstruction committee and the US Army Engineers in coordination with the Secretariat of the National Assembly. Hellmuth, Obata and Kassabaum (HOK), New York office, reconstruct interiors, 1991–92, with Juliette Lam designer in charge.

NOV 28   **Professor H. Ingham Ashworth** dies aged 84.

1992

JAN 22   Media announcement that Jørn Utzon, Frank O. Gehry and Sir Denys Lasdun have been awarded the **Wolf Foundation Prize in Arts (Architecture)**. The prize is worth US$100,000 with the award ceremony in Jerusalem. The Wolf Foundation was established by Ricardo Wolf, a German–born inventor, in 1975. In Utzon's case, the award recognised *'qualities existing well beyond the range of passing fashion, qualities that enhance use, transform construction and liberate the mind.'*

MAY Wolf Prize is presented to Utzon in a ceremony in Jerusalem. His citation reads: *'His architecture, rooted in a deep reading of human cultures, has given shape to processes of ritual and assembly of forms of haunting presence.'*

JUNE 30 Opera House Trust spends $3.9 million on SOH improvements in the year 1991–92.

OCT The restoration of Kuwait National Assembly is completed in October for a total cost of K.D. 19,394,705.

OCT 5 New Majlis is elected and convenes on 20 Oct, 1992. The National Assembly Building was repaired and back in service in time for the new Majlis to sit.

1993

MAR 4 Thursday: a bronze plaque honouring Jørn Utzon is unveiled at SOH by daughter Lin in the presence of the **Hon. Peter Collins**, Minister for the Arts. In correspondence between SOHT and Utzon, Utzon insisted the plaque not be about himself but should be a demonstration of the spherical solution.

MAR 17 Underground car park for SOH with capacity for 1,100 cars is opened officially by the John Joseph Fahey (b. 1945–, NSW Premier and Treasurer 1992–95); the cost exceeds A$40 million.

JUNE 30 In 1992–93, SOH Trust spends $1.887 million on maintaining the Opera House.

AUG 8 Sunday: **Steph Beaumont** (Lin Utzon's 2nd husband) dies after a stroke following a prolonged illness.

DEC 31 Total expenditure on Upgrade Program 1 for SOH at 22 Dec, 1993, $60.753 million; John Zaat (PWD) in charge as Project Manager.

1994

'Can Feliz' Utzon's 2nd House, is completed in 1995 (1992–95) in Sierra del Levante mountains behind Alqueria del Blanca on south–eastern coast of Majorca. The house is sited below a ruined Moorish castle.

Pi Michael, Danish radio journalist, completes television documentary titled *Skyer* (Clouds) about Utzon's architecture and design for Danish Radio. Her dedication to producing a documentary on Utzon led to her sacking because of a cost overrun.

JAN *Sydney Opera House Travelling Exhibition*, curated by Paul Bentley, is sent to Australian Embassy, Paris (Jan. '94); Rome Opera House; Olivanderhof, Cologne; Kennedy Centre as part of Kennedy Centre Festival Australia; Amagasaki Cultural Centre, Japan; Seoul Arts Centre (Dec.'95)

APR 8 Premier of *Tanne* by Nyt Dansk Dansteater with scenography designed by Lin Utzon.

JUNE 30 In 1993–94, Sydney Opera House Trust spends $2.336 million on repairs and maintenance (see *Annual Report*).

SEPT **Poul Nyrup Rasmussen and his Social Democratic Party win 62 of the 179 seats in the Folketing, the single chamber parliament in the general election.**

SEPT 11 *Jørn Utzon Udvalgte Arbejder, 1942–1988*, exhibition at Skissernas Museum, finngatan 2, Lund, Sweden, from 11 Sep–23 Oct. 1994.

NOV 1 *The Unseen Utzon* exhibition of the unbuilt Sydney Opera House interiors, curated by John Murphy, presented at SOH Exhibition Hall from Nov 1, 1994 to June 30, 1995. Philip Nobis' highly effective computer imaging of the interiors is seen by 25,500 visitors.

DEC 4 SOH Improvements (State Government funded $120 Million Upgrade Programme no. 1 (first), including maintenance begun in 1988):

Tile lids weatherproofed (completed 1994)–$6.5 million;

Opera Theatre Orchestra Pit area enlarged, floor lowered and acoustics improved (just completed) — cost $690,000 to build, plus an additional $150,000 in electronic work, total cost $840,000;

Granite ceremonial forecourt stairs — removed to allow for new waterproofing, and then rebuilt (completed 1993);

Opera Theatre shut down for 35 days in 1991/92 to enable extensive work including refurbishment of auditorium air conditioning. Shut down again in November 1994 to allow work on pit floors, lighting, and winch flying system;

Glass walls: replace rusted sub–sill supports and resealed;

Broadwalk around Bennelong Point, constant maintenance on concrete column supports due to salt water corrosion. Multi–million dollar refurbishment planned.

Cafe Mozart extended, with coffee bar replacing half of Concert Hall cloak room.

All 5,000 seats replaced with new multi–cushioned ones (completed in 1993), cost more than $5 million or $1,000 a seat.

Performing Arts Museum to be opened in 1997, called Theatreworks, and Concert Hall Backstage Assembly area to be located under Concert Hall.

Forecourt & Lower Concourse arcade: major remodelling and new construction of lower concourse including arcade with shops, restaurant.

1995

JAN 12	Lillian Waerum (Hojgaarden) proposes a new museum on Samsø Island to be designed by Jørn Utzon.
MAR 21	Lin Utzon presents the 1965 scale model of the Main Hall to the Sydney Opera House Trust represented by Peter Collins. Lin says, on behalf of Utzon, it was *'The dream that came to life.'*
MAR 25	**The Labor Party, led by Robert John Carr (b. 1947–), a former journalist, is elected replacing the Fahey Coalition government on 4 April: ALP 50, Nats 17, Lib 29 (46 total), Ind 3 (99 seats).**
APR 15	**Mr Robert McNamara, former US Defence Secretary, says that and he and his colleagues were wrong, *'terribly wrong'* to have carried fighting in Vietnam for as long as they did.**
MAY 19	Friday: **Peter Brian Hall** (b. Newcastle 1931), dies after a short illness following a stroke aged 64. The funeral service was at the North Sydney Crematorium. Suffering from alcoholism, a series of professional setbacks culminating in the collapse of his architectural practice in early 1990s with large debts, his health gave way.
JUNE 30	The SOH Trust spends $5.472 million on repairs and maintenance during 1994–95 according to the *Annual Report.*
AUG 23	Wednesday: the Bennelong Restaurant $1.3 million refit by Gay Bilson, Leigh Prentice and Anders Ousbach opens with seating for 100.
AUG 25	Friday: announcement of submission costing $200,000 for **World Heritage listing to go before the UNESCO World Heritage Committee, Paris,** by NSW Minister for Urban Affairs and Planning funded by the Federal Government through its Federal Environment Minister, Hon Senator John Faulkner.

OCT 7 2 projects: culture/history and art museum proposed for Stavn Fjord on Samsø island, 150,000 kr ($A 30,000) advanced with sketch proposal; Skagen Museum at Grenen with large and small lecture rooms, rooms for meetings, music, exhibitions, garden, and 14m cube room with niche and northern viewing window. Jørn in association with Kim Utzon. Intended to be completed by mid–1998.

OCT 14 World première *The Eighth Wonder*, an opera composed by Alan John with libretto by Dennis Watkins, in the Opera Theatre of SOH. Utzon is played by David Hobson. The two–act opera was commissioned by the Australian Opera after a two–day workshop at its Surry Hills headquarters and performance of a 40 minute excerpt in October 1992. It explores the epic drama and controversial building of the Sydney Opera House.

1996

MARCH The Lord Mayor of Sydney, **Councillor Sartor**, visits Utzon to inform him about developments in the Circular Quay controversy.

Keating government offers Colonial Mutual Life $180 million to buy out East Circular Quay site immediately before the March 1996 federal election. A further offer of $30 million to lower the height by 5–storeys is rejected by the company.

MAY 22 Hon Robert J. Carr, NSW Premier, tables correspondence between the Hon Sir Davis Hughes, Minister for Public Works and Jørn Utzon in the NSW Parliament and announces an allocation in the budget of $68,000 towards the preservation of the State Library of NSW's *Jørn Utzon collection*. Archives Authority of New South Wales releases records relating to the resignation of Jørn Utzon from Sydney Opera House under the 30–year rule.

JUNE Los Angeles: **Jose Raphael Moneo** receives the US$100,000 Pritzker Architecture Prize, the world's most prestigious architecture honour. As an assistant in Utzon's Hellebæk team, Moneo made the spherical geometry roof drawings for the SOH. The same month as the award, he was chosen to design the new $50 million Catholic cathedral in Los Angeles.

JUNE 20 Thursday: Federal Minister for Environment and Sport, Senator Robert Hill (Liberal, South Australia), Australian Federal Parliament, Canberra, delays consideration of World Heritage documents by one week to consider financial aspects of listing, results in a late submission to UNESCO after deadline for applications has passed, delaying the bid a year.

JUNE 30 SOH Upgrade Program 1 expenditure in 1995–96 is $9,656,000. According to its *Annual Report*, the SOH Trust also spent $8.257 million on repairs and maintenance to the Opera House.

JULY 8	Lionel Todd puts forward proposal to build a new State Opera Theatre south of the Museum of Contemporary Art to replace the main hall of the SOH, a 2 to 3 storey building on Circular Quay East on the CML site and a commercial and residential building next to the Cahill Expressway which would be covered by a link building in front of the railway station. Circular Quay to be returned to a semi–circular shaped basin.
JULY 25	Thursday: Deputy Premier, NSW state government, forwards nomination to Canberra, but tensions continue between the federal (Lib/Nat) and state (Labor) governments. The July 1 deadline for the nomination to UNESCO is extended till July 25. Its further extension to 1997 carries the risk of changes in the UNESCO guidelines.
AUG 5	Monday: 7 p.m., Atlanta 1996 Olympics closing ceremony. At climax of Sydney 2000 presentation in main stadium for the Games of the XXVII Olympiad, giant white spars are raised represent the sails of the Sydney Opera House — icon of the 2000 Games.
AUG 7	Wednesday: The Federal Government announces it will not proceed with the Opera House nomination for World Heritage this year.
OCT	Dennis Wolanski Library of the Performing Arts is closed and its archive is dispersed to the University of New South Wales Librart and other locations; Paul Bentley, librarian–in–charge, leaves SOH after 24 years.
DEC	Peter Knowland, an acoustics expert who worked as an assistant to Vilhelm Jordan (1957 – 82), submits a report on the SOH's acoustics, based on comments by two overseas acoustics experts, Karlheinz Muller and Larry Kirkegaad.

1997

	Musikhuset in Esbjerg, by Jørn Utzon with Jan and Kim, opens for the winter season.
FEB 14	Friday: 12 noon, FIRST PROTEST RALLY against MLC re–development of Circular Quay East arranged by Neville Gruzman; 3,000 attend in the rain.
MAR 17	David Lloyd Martin (b. Apr 30, 1934–) retires after almost 18 years as General Manager of SOH (1979–77). Previously, he was Deputy General Manager from 1973–79. Martin is replaced by the influential Victorian arts bureaucrat, Mr Tim Jacobs (b. 1951–). The Opera House was reeling from a management restructuring, a staff of more than 400, and a firmly entrenched workplace culture plagued by industrial action over its 25–year history.
MAR 22	Submission for World Heritage Listing by UNESCO is rejected by Federal Cabinet on the grounds that the Bennelong Development had stymied the proposal according to Senator Hill, Federal Environment Minister.
MAR 25	Tuesday 3.20 pm: **Phillip Norman Ryan** dies.

> **RYAN**
> Norman Ryan (b. 24 May, 1912 at Moruya, d. 25 March 1997) was appointed by Labor Premier J.J. Cahill as Minister for Public Works from 1959 to May 1965. In opposition he did his best to support Utzon. He lived in retirement at Killarny Vale on the Central Coast and died the week before Easter aged 84. He and is survived by wife Dorothy Ryan, children Desmond and Lynette, and grandsons of Phillip and David.

MARCH 26   Elias Duek–Cohen approaches Utzon (Hellebæk) about preliminary talks with the NSW Ministry for the Arts to update Utzon's SOH drawings using Mogens Prip–Buus, Oktay Nayman, and Joachim Nutsch.

MAR 27   Second release of *SYDNEY OPERA HOUSE DOCUMENTS 1966–1976* by the Archives Authority of New South Wales. Items released include Review of Programme, glass walls, car park, cost blow–out, the organ, value for money and attendance statistics 1994–5 & 1995–96.

APR 1   SOH Masterplan (UG2) process begins under a Control Group led by Chris Johnson, NSWGA at NSW Public Works Department; to take 7 months.

APR 6   Sunday from 12 to 5: SECOND RALLY AGAINST CIRCULAR QUAY EAST DEVELOPMENT; speakers include Doug Sutherland, Sonia Fenton, Jack Mundey, Ted Mack with entertainment provided by Mick Conway and Whoopie Band — 3,500 attend.

APR 9   Wednesday: Elias Duek–Cohen writes a second letter to Utzon at Hellebæk encouraging him to consider his proposal and suggests that Bill Wheatland visit him to talk about updating SOH.

APR 15   Utzon replies to Elias Duek–Cohen (from Cala D'Or, Mallorca): *'But as to your idea of rebuilding SOH I am utterly negative. It is impossible! For various reasons, first of all the structure of the shells and the base might be destroyed in various places during demolition.'* Utzon suggests instead that *'the NSW Government build a new opera house elsewhere and keep the SOH, leaving the Major and Minor Halls as they are now, but use the Minor Hall as a theatre only with its small orchestra pit level introducing the original revolving stage with its two elevators.'* He further writes: *'I do not think anybody with knowledge of the SOH construction would take the responsibility of recommending to the Government, that it would be economically sensible or technically possible to tear down and rebuild.'*

APR 29   Duek–Cohen writes for a third time to Utzon.

MAY 17   Utzon replies to Duek–Cohen (from Cala D'Or, Mallorca): *'I do not want my drawings for the interiors and the glass walls to be finished or worked on in any way or by any one. It is not feasible! No visits from Bill [W.W. Wheatland] or from any friend will alter this point of view of mine.'*

MAY 29	Mr David Brice, a Hong Kong and Los Angeles property developer, finalises an option on the Royal Automobile Club (RAC) site and later floats proposal to amalgamate the RAC and the Quay Apartments in a single tower into which the Hong Kong and Shanghai Hotels Corporation (HKSHC) would transfer apartments from its contentious Circular Quay site.
JUNE	Launch of the Cultural Cooperation Project 'Denmark Meets Australia' in Copenhagen by the Danish Government with $300,000 given in support for the Barossa Music Festival from Oct. 4–19. Events in Sydney, Canberra, Melbourne and Barossa Valley, S.A., during October. Architectural event is planned to coincide with the 25th anniversary of the completion of the SOH on 20 October 1998.
JUNE 30	SOH Upgrade Program 1 expenditure in 1996–97 is $11,836,000 (of this $7,278,000 is paid for from a state government grant). Total expenditure on repairs and maintenance to the building during 1996–97 is $12,221,000. The SOH Trust paid NSW Public Works as Project Manager, $7,278,000 for the management and execution of the Upgrade Program. Budgeted expenditure for 30 June 1998 set at $9,570,000. The State Government indicates its supports for an upgrade program involving an outlay of $117 million over a period of 10 years.
JULY 9	4th letter by Duek–Cohen to Utzon expresses his disappointment at Utzon's rejection of his proposal.
AUG 7	Thursday: Colonial Peninsula Pty Ltd (subsidiary of Hong Kong and Shanghai Hotels (HKSH)) development application for a new 11–storey 228 bed hotel to cost $170 million including retail, restaurant, bar and cafe areas, rehearsal and administrative offices for the Australian Chamber Orchestra, arthouse cinemas and parking for 211 cars at Circular Quay East site approved by the Central City Council Planning Committee (CSPC) at end of a hostile 2 hour debate at which a petition of more than 45,000 signatures against the development was submitted. The amended development application is lodged by the owners after a decision in May to jettison construction of 140 apartments and replace them with a luxury hotel.
AUG 31	**Sunday: Princess Diana dies at 36 early Sunday morning together with Dodi Fayed (41) and French driver after a car crash in Paris.**
SEPT 8	Monday: 5,000 Royal Automobile Club members vote to decide whether to accept David Brice's two stage $19 million offer to develop air rights above the historic Macquarie Street property.
SEPT 9	Tuesday: 77% of the members reject the Brice proposal as inadequate following an independent assessment.
SEPT 10	Wednesday. night: The chief executive of HKSH, Mr Pierre Boppe, confirms that despite gaining development approval from city authorities just 3 weeks earlier on August 7, a hotel does not appear to be economically viable and a quick sale of the luxury apartments would yield a greater financial return. The Minister for Planning, Mr Knowles is informed of the decision the same day (Wed).

SEPT 11   Chairman of the Save East Circular Quay Committee, Mr Jack Mundey, calls for a summit to resolve the fate of the ECQ development.

SEPT 19   **Mr Tim Jacobs** (former director of Arts Victoria (1995–97), now chief executive of SOH, announces a 2nd Upgrade of costing $35 million which includes Leif Kristensen's proposal for a Western Broadwalk Foyer, linking the Drama Theatre, new Broadwalk Studio and Playhouse on Circular Quay side, ultimately intended to connect with box office foyer (UG2).

OCT 10   Australian debut of the New Danish Dance Theatre production, 'Tanne' opens at the newly completed Langbein Theatre at the Barossa Music Festival. Choreography by Warren Spears, to a score by Fuzzy inspired by Karen Blixen's writings Out of Africa. The production was designed by Lin Utzon.

OCT 16, 17, & 18   3 performances of *'Tanne'* at the Newtown Theatre, 354 King Street, Newtown, during Newtown Festival.

OCT 20   Lin Utzon leaves Denmark for Mallorca to visit her parents Jørn & Lis on Mallorca.

OCT 27   **Monday: New York Stock Exchange, Dow Jones index plunges 554.26 points (down 7.18%). The All Ordinaries in Australia down 177.8 (7.29%) follows. Tuesday, NY Market recovers 332 points.**

OCT 29   Wednesday: **Herbert Cole Coombs** dies aged 91.

> **COOMBS**
> Herbert Coombs (b. Feb 24, 1906–d. 1997), educated at Perth Modern School, University of WA, was instrumental in setting up the Elizabethan Theatre Trust and was its Chairman from 1954 to 1968; indirectly in this role, was involved in the controversy after Utzon on the use of the Main Hall of the SOH.

NOV 1   Masterplan as it currently exists is signed off (UG2).

NOV 3   Monday: Elias Duek–Cohen and William Wheatland meet Tim Jacobs (SOH CEO) and Chris Johnson (NSW Government Architect) for discussion of possibility of updating Utzon's SOH drawings using former staff members such as Mogens Prip–Buus. Utzon remains opposed.

NOV 10   Publication by David Messent of *Opera House Act One*. History of SOH construction 1778 to tiles, mainly from Ove Arup & Partners' viewpoint.

NOV 19   Wednesday. Mr. Scully, the Minister for Public Works and Services, announces that the original matt tiles on the edges of the tile lids of SOH roof are to be replaced in January 1998 with 5,600 new matching tiles supplied by The Remedial Engineering Pty Ltd, Rydalmere, NSW, under a contract taking 70 weeks and costing $6.5 million.

Work also starts on the construction of the new Broadwalk Studio for the SOH, located between the Playhouse and the Drama Theatre. It will have a performance space seating 330.

NOV 28   Friday.: $3 million to be spent upgrading lighting under a proposal by Lighting Design Partnership for 18,000 new lights inside and outside to replace the existing exterior lights which were installed in 1988, and original 1973 interior lights, to illuminate the entire Bennelong Point site.

DEC 7   Sunday afternoon: **Mr Bob Carr**, NSW Premier unveils a $66.59 million Masterplan in two stages to upgrade (UG2) the SOH over ten years to a crowd of 30,000 attending a concert of opera selections on the forecourt steps.

SECOND SOH UPGRADE IN TWO STAGES

Stage 1 ($32.05 million) for completion in time for the 2000 Olympic Games, to be funded from the Commonwealth Government's $1 billion Federation Fund and comprising: the full cost of the pre–2000 construction, including the new State funded $9.5 million Broadwalk Studio with a capacity of 370 to be completed by December 1998, which has already been approved, is $41.55 million (Leif Kristensen & Partners paid $53,925 for accommodation review, and $134,300 for Broadwalk Studio project — June '97).

Stage 2 ($34.54 million), post 2000 component, to be funded by the NSW state government ($7.57million).

DEC 12   Friday: **Professor Kenneth Frampton** suggests that the only way to redeem the damage done to Circular Quay East is to widen the causeway linking the SOH to the Quay and recommends that a moratorium be placed on the rest of the row of buildings, and the developer compensated. He opines that the Opera House is a far more significant building than the new and much–hailed [Bilbao] Guggenheim museum in Spain by the architect Frank Gehry: *'Gehry's masterpiece in my opinion is a much weaker work, nowhere near as significant as the Opera House, a piece of large sculpture not really a building at all, not architecture at all, whereas the Opera House is a building, a piece of tectonic work.'*

1998

JAN 3   Saturday. Sydney Festival, 30 high–intensity floodlights (costing $160,000) are used to paint the Opera House Kline blue for the 22nd Sydney Festival, designed by lighting designer Alan Stone until Jan. 26.

JAN 7   Letter from UNESCO sent to the Australian Ambassador in Paris, Mr John Spender, warns that the $500 million East Circular Quay project may contravene UNESCO's World Heritage Listing rules. It states that developments which 'jeopardise the character of the site in accordance with criteria for the World Heritage Listing should be avoided.' The SOH remains tentatively listed for World Heritage registration despite Federal Cabinet's vote in March 1997 against forwarding the nomination.

JAN 9 Friday: the World Première of *Complicity*, a play by Timothy Daly about Eugene Goossens conviction on charges of importing pornography in 1956 opens at the Marian Street Theatre, Killara, with Angela Punch McGregor, Barbara Stephens, John Allen, Bill Charlton, David Baldwin, Matthew Jackson, & David Downer. It ran until Jan 22.

FEB Utzon rejects any participation in the SOH Upgrade program by himself and asks Alex Popov to keep his involvement to a minimum.

Jørn and son Kim Utzon visit the Louisiana Art Museum at Humlebæk to discuss with the museum founder, Knud W. Jensen. His proposal for a new Museum of Architecture addition is sited below on the shore north of the present museum.

February issue of *The Architectural Review* (London) condemns the East Circular Quay development as 'sad and banal', and a 'monster of international significance.'

FEB 4 Expressions of Interest: Tenders invited for implementing the Sydney Opera House Masterplan UG2 which sets out a ten year strategy for the building and site improvements. Tenders to close 5 p.m. Friday 20 Feb.

FEB 10 Tuesday briefing session on UG2 tenders at 1 p.m. in the Reception Hall. Presentation by Tim Jacobs (CEO), John McWhinney (Director Property Services) & John Dare (Manager, Facilities Planning).

FEB 20 Friday, UG2 submission of Tenders. 22 received most from project managers, only 5 are from architects.

FEB 21 Save East Circular Quay web site launched at www.savethequay.org.au

FEB 22 Lionel Todd dies of cancer. No obituary or formal notice in papers or by Royal Australian Institute of Architects. He is survived by his wife Margaret Todd.

FEB 23 Monday, UG2 selection of Tenders.

FEB 28 Saturday. Tim Jacobs resigns as General Manager and Chief Executive of the SOH after less than a year in the post and returns to Melbourne as General Manager of the Victorian Arts Centre.

MAR 2 UG2, briefing of selected Consultants completed.

Yuzo Mikami visits Sydney until 12 March; appointments with Tim Jacobs (CEO SOH Trust), Mary Valentine (GM SSO), Noel Staunton (Technical Director, Opera Australia) to talk about the Upgrading Program. Also plans to meet Leif Kristensen, engineers at OA & P involved in the re–tiling of the shell–roofs.

MAR 9	Monday: Upgrade short list is judged by Daryl Jackson, Chris Johnson, and James Grose, who whittle list of 5 or 6 down to three firms: Richard Johnson (Denton Corker Marshall), Keith Cottier (Allen Jack + Cottier) in association with George Freedman, and Richard Francis Jones (Mitchell/Giurgola & Thorp).
MAR 11	**Wednesday: Snap election called by Danish Prime Minister Poul Nyrup Rasmussen to be fought on the future shape of the European Union and on immigration policy. Denmark was the only EU member to vote against the Maastricht Treaty in 1992. The Government, with the support of the Radical Party won 90 seats, beats Opposition led by Mr Uffe Ellemann–Jensen with 89 seats; to retain office with a 1 seat majority in the 179 seat Folketing.**
MAR 13	UG2: first submissions by consultants.
MAR 16	UG2: presentations by consultants to SOH Trust commence.
MAR 17	Tuesday: The Lord Mayor of Sydney, Councillor Sartor, launches booklet by Ms Shirley Fitzgerald, *East Circular Quay 1788–1998* (32pp) published at a cost of $20,000.
MAR 30	UG2: SOHT approves architect consultant.
MAR 31	Save East Circular Quay Committee appeals to the federal government to reverse the desecration of the Sydney Opera House environs.
APR 3	Announcement of the selection of consultants for UG2. This was to be finalised in early April, but is extended.
APR 3	Friday: Jan Utzon leaves Denmark to join his parents on Mallorca for Utzon's birthday celebrations the following week.
APR 6	Monday: Councillor Sartor, the Mayor of Sydney, announces that Utzon has accepted the award of 'the keys of the City of Sydney'. Council approved award by a unanimous vote.
APR 9	Thursday: Utzon celebrates his 80th birthday on Mallorca, Spain.
MID–APR	SOH Accommodation Review is completed.
APR 16	Thursday: Lecture by Elias Duek–Cohen, 'Jørn Utzon and the Sydney Opera House,' at UTS, 6 p.m. to celebrate Utzon's birthday.
APR 17	**Friday: Utzon is awarded Denmark's prestigious Sonning Prize** which carries a monetary prize of 500,000 DK kr. ($A 111,000) on Mr Sonning's birthday at Copenhagen University. Utzon is welcomed by the Rector, Kjeld Møllgard, in the old Festival Hall, peroration delivered by Prof Carsten Thau for *'an outstanding contribution toward the advancement of European Civilization,'* after which, Utzon is presented with award and cheque which he drops on the floor, then makes a short speech of thanks from lectern. The ceremony is witnessed by Kulture Minister, Elsebeth Gerner Nielsen, and there is extensive coverage in newspapers and television.

Jørn Utzon receiving the Sonning prize by Erik Werner

APR 17	*Utzon: Portræt af den danske arkitekt Jørn Utzon 1942–1995* (Portrait of the Danish architect Jørn Utzon) exhibition at Rejsestaldene, Halmtorvet 9A, 1700 København V opens, it runs till 1 June. Curated by Jes Vagnby with photographs by Flemming Bo Andersen.
APR 30	Thursday. Denton Corker Marshall (Melbourne) is chosen as the preferred architect for the $66.5 M UG2. Richard Johnson is most involved. .
MAY 7	Thursday: E. Duek–Cohen telephones Kim Utzon about the Utzon Foundation; speaks to Jørn Utzon, who agrees to the idea of the Utzon Foundation in the form of an international performing arts prize.
MAY 8	Friday, 9.00 a.m.: E. Duek–Cohen has meeting on the Utzon Foundation proposal with Barbara Tiernan, Jane Westbrook (SOHT), and Gianfranco Cresciani (Ministry for the Arts). Tim Jacobs leaves the SOH to take up position as GM at the Victorian Arts Centre, Melbourne.
MAY 12	Tuesday: Federal government budget 1998: no Federal money is allocated to SOH Upgrade; instead, Federation Fund money is to be used as a slush fund by the Liberal Party to buy votes in the upcoming federal election.
MAY 13	Wednesday: Evan Williams flies to Copenhagen for meeting with Jørn Utzon in Kim Utzon's office to discuss the Utzon Foundation proposal.
MAY 20	Wednesday 7 p.m.: public meeting, Lower Town Hall, organised by the SECQ Committee is attended by 1,300 protestors, who demand the East Circular Quay building be pulled down. It is addressed by 11 speakers including Dr Tim Flannery, Margaret Throsby, and ICAC Commissioner Mr Barry O'Keefe, QC.
MAY 21	Thursday: In a *Politiken* interview, Utzon comments: *'When you fly over Australia you can see that there is plenty of land but the cities crowd together with high density and enormous skyscrapers; so that it is as if [one has] moved into a big house yet all the furniture is in one room.*
	Now, one [developer] is also building high–rise close to the Opera House. It would be like building a gigantic apartment block in the Garden of Amaliehaven next to the Palace Amalienborg....
	The money will quickly be earned back on the investment but the place is destroyed forever.' 'Hovedstad eller hunderkirkegard,' *Politiken*, Sun, 29 March 1998, p. 5 (translated by Lin Utzon).
MAY 28	**Thursday: Danes vote in a referendum on whether Denmark is to join the European Union. Result, 55.1 per cent "yes" and "no" side 44.9 per cent, paves the way for the European Union's eastern expansion. (Denmark has 5.3 million people compared with Europe's combined population of 370 million or 1.43%).**
JUNE 5	Friday: Utzon telephones Melbourne documentary film maker Daryl Dellora at his hotel in Copenhagen and later gives a full day interview at his forest home at Hellebæk: *'This is an Australian building that should be cared for at this time in Australian history, when your country is at the end of the colony of Australia and at*

the beginning of the Republic of Australia. The spirit of this building is independent of anything anywhere. It is 100 per cent Australian. This [the listing] and the Year 2000 fit beautifully together. Then you can hear beautiful music all the time in the future from a clean well–kept building. Please tell them in Canberra — Help!'

JUNE 8   'Five for the Ages,' *Time magazine*, no. 23, June 8, 1998, p. 69 chose the SOH with the Chrysler Building (1930), Seagram Building (1958), Hong Kong and Shanghai Bank (1985) and Guggenheim Bilbao Museum (1987) as the five most important buildings of the 20th century.

JUNE 10   Wednesday morning: speaking on ABC Radio, the **Prime Minister John Howard**, rejects a proposal to use $200 million of Federation Fund money to buy back the East Circular Quay site, saying that it is purely a state government matter. Kim Beazely agrees. Howard also confirms that the Federal Government will not forward the nomination of the Opera House for a World Heritage listing despite the call by the International Union of Architects representing more than 100 countries. On 2BL, Mr Howard says: *'I don't think there is any particular reason for or against [the nomination]…It's not going to…alter the status of the Opera House. It is not going to alter it as a focal point of tourist attraction…I am not ruling it out forever but…you don't automatically list every single thing.'*

JUNE 30   Tuesday: Expiry of deadline for Opera House nomination to the World Heritage Register. John Howard PM fails to forward the SOH nomination.

JULY 1   Wednesday: **Mr Michael Lynch** is appointed chief executive officer of the SOH. To take appointment in early September.

> **LYNCH**
> Michael Lynch (b. 6 Dec 1951–) was previously general manager and chief executive of the Australia Council 1994–98, the Federal Arts funding body. Studied Arts/Law at University of Sydney but dropped out before completing degree (1969–72). Mr Lynch was GM of the Nimrod Theatre (1976–78) and GM of the Sydney Theatre Company (1989–94).

JULY 8   Wednesday: Alderman Frank Sartor, Lord Mayor of Sydney, meets Jørn Utzon at a restaurant at S'Horta near Can Feliz on Mallorca and hands him the key to Sydney. In a handwritten thank–you letter Utzon says: *'My years with Sydney Opera House were the most wonderful in my architectural life.'*

JULY 21   Tuesday: Mr Pierre Boppe, chief executive of Hong Kong shanghai Hotels writes to Prime Minister Mr Howard confirming that the company is willing to demolish the East Circular Quay apartment complex and states that the Peninsular luxury hotel chain has continued enthusiasm to build a hotel and asks for economic assistance.

AUG 27	Thursday: **Mr Harry Jensen**, Sydney's longest serving Lord Mayor (1956–65), dies in Prince of Wales Hospital, Randwick, aged 85. He was the MLA for Wyong from 1965 and retired from state politics in 1981.
SEPT 1	Monday: Chairman of the SOH Trust, Mr Joe Skrzynski, announces the appointment of **Denton Corker Marshall (DCM)** to prepare new guidelines for a 25–year masterplan for SOH. DCM has been asked to look at the Bennelong Point precinct in its entirety. Mr Richard Johnson, a principal of DCM, says their first task will be to research archival material to establish Utzon's vision for the Opera House and East Circular Quay.
OCT 3	Saturday: a month–long celebration (3–31 Oct.) for the SOH's 25th birthday begins with *Pelleas & Melisande*, Debussy's only opera, accompanied by an exhibition of Lin Utzon ceramics in the Southern Foyer of the Concert Hall to 25 Oct.
OCT 18	Sunday, 3 p.m.: screening of Film Art Doco's film *The Edge of the Possible* about Jørn Utzon launched by Harry Seidler in the Reception Hall SOH.
OCT 19	Monday 10:30 a.m.: the Premier of NSW, Mr Bob Carr, to coincide with the 25th anniversary of the completion of the SOH announces, in the Bennelong Restaurant, the formation of the Utzon Foundation. It will award a $100,000 biennial prize for outstanding achievement in the performing arts. The Foundation is sponsored by the NSW Ministry for the Arts, the City of Sydney and the SOH Trust.

Utzon sends message: *'In the 25 years of its existence, the Sydney Opera House has been a marvellous and inseparable part of my life. I am gratified that it should be seen by its trustees and by the Government and people of New South Wales as a fitting symbol of the standard of creative excellence which the Foundation will seek to inspire.'*

5–6:30 p.m.: exhibition viewing of Lin Utzon Porcelain, curated by Martin Sharp.

OCT 20	Tuesday 8:30 p.m. on ABC TV: Screening of The Daryl Dellora documentary, *The Edge of the Possible* (1966–98).

10:30pm: cocktail gala function in the Northern Foyer of the Concert Hall to mark 25 years from the official opening of the SOH is attended by Mr Joe Skryzynski, Mr Michael Lynch, Mr and Mrs Carr, Governor and Chief Justice of NSW. Lin Utzon's reply to Mr Carr speech is followed by a video message from Jørn Utzon lasting 5 minutes on the big screen under the seating ramp. Michael Lynch introduces a film reviewing 25 years of performances in SOH. Drinks and music follow.

OCT 23	Friday: the Premier Mr Carr sends an offer in writing to Jørn Utzon for him to serve as the principal consultant to the Sydney Opera House Trust for the renewal and modification of the interior of the Opera House. The offer will be delivered to Mr Utzon at his home in Mallorca, Spain, personally by Mr Richard Johnson (DCM), who has been engaged by the NSW government to prepare a 10–year masterplan.

OCT 25   Sunday: at a performance of operatic arias outside the Opera House presented by Opera Australia, Sydney Opera House Trust and *Sydney Morning Herald*, Mr Carr announces his offer to Utzon:

'My Government shares [the view] with the people of Sydney, who feel a sense of profound loss and regret when recalling the circumstances of your departure 32 years ago. We regret especially that the architect who conceived this great project was not here to complete it.

'It is clear that while the Opera House will stand for centuries to come, its interiors will from time to time need renewal or modification for technical and functional reasons.

'These tasks, together with any other work undertaken by future governments, will be greatly assisted by the development of a comprehensive and enduring statement of design principles. It is our fervent wish that such a statement of principle should faithfully reflect your vision and meet with your approval.'

NOV 5   Jones Lang Wooton opens two showroom apartments at 1 Macquarie Street for inspection. Prices range from $800,000 for a studio apartment to $6 million for a four–bedroom penthouse suite. One Macquarie Street is the first stage of the project's $750 million 237 apartments, which will include a 700–seat arthouse cinema, up to 25 fashion stores and nine eateries along the two–storey, 200 metre–long granite colonnade. Rents are as high as $3,500 per m². 58 apartments have been sold since 1995 and contracts exchanged on 37 after Bennelong had been put on the market two weeks previously. Mr Keith Hutchence, for the Save East Circular Quay Committee, concedes the development would never be pulled down.

NOV 9   Monday: **Sir Asher Joel**, dies.

> **JOEL**
> Asher Joel, KBE, Kt, AO (b. Sydney 4 May 1912–9 Nov 1998) organised the official opening of the Sydney Opera House in 1973 and was appointed by Cahill to the SOH Executive Committee.

NOV 13   The Song Company finishes performing at the Musikhuset at Esjberg, Denmark. Eugene Ragghianti (Company Manager) comments that the acoustics are 'Utter bliss'.

NOV 16   Tuesday: **George Molnar** dies, aged 88.

DEC 1   Tuesday: Mr Bob Debus, the Minister Assisting the Premier, launches the inaugural season of the $12 million Studio performance venue at SOH. It is scheduled for completion on 5 March 1999. Designed by Leif Kristensen, construction of the new space began in 1997. It has a 15 m² performance floor, flexible four–sided seating plan, a mechanically variable acoustic system, 36–channel lighting desk and adjoining recording studio.

DEC 4   Friday: Peter Collins is replaced as parliamentary Leader of the Opposition Liberal Party by Mrs Kerry Chikarovski.

1999

JAN 26   Plans for a Museum of Architecture to be built on the shore below the Lousiana Museum of Modern Art by Jørn Utzon and Kim Utzon are unveiled. The 900 m² museum, connected to the existing museum via an underground tunnel, would command impressive views of the waterway separating Denmark from Sweden. Whether or not the project proceeds will depend on finding a satisfactory and acceptable solution to the acute traffic and parking problem caused by Lousiana. Knud W. Jensen, Lousiana's founder, claims the museum is needed because Denmark lacks an architectural museum. 13 million people have visited Louisiana Museum since it opened in 1958, 40 years ago. The visitor figure in 1998 was 425,000 compared with 410,000 in 1986, 540,000 in 1996, and a record of 640,000 for the year 1994.

FEB 24   Jørn Utzon agrees to write design prescriptions and assist as a consultant with the refurbishment of the SOH. Jan Utzon is quoted as saying, *'the Opera House should be a living thing; it shouldn't be a fixed thing.'*

MAR 5   Friday: Costing $12 million and seating 364, predominantly red with natural wood finishes by architect Leif Kristensen, 'The Studio' opens with performances by Sprung Percussion.

MAR 23   Tuesday: Construction Industry Manufacturers' Association at its Construction Exhibition at Las Vegas USA votes the SOH one of the ten top construction achievements of the 20th century, a list which includes the Aswan Dam, the Channel Tunnel, Golden Gate bridge.

MAR 27   **Saturday: Carr Labor government in NSW re–elected with 53.7 per cent of the vote, an increased majority, and a 4.9 per cent swing across NSW. State of the parties in the new parliament: ALP 53, Liberal 21, National 13 (total 34), Independents 6. The result will ensure that the plans for SOH made in 1998 will be implemented.**

MAY   Carr government sends letter to the Prime Minister asking the federal government to support the nomination of the SOH for World Heritage status by June 30. The government in Canberra has refused to make a nomination in 1996, 1997, and 1998, giving as its reason it does not want to be liable for any costs arising from a World Heritage listing and concerns that the Commonwealth may face demands to intervene in Sydney Harbour management issues. The letter asserts:

'World Heritage listing would be a signal honour for one whose vision has given so much to the performing arts in Australia and our nation's cultural development.'

JUNE 15   **Mr Edo de Waart**, chief conductor of the SSO, complains in ABC Radio's *24 Hours magazine* the SOH Concert Hall detracted from the SSO's sound and described the 'doughnuts', as a 'joke' which might as well be toilet seats. Ms Mary Valentine, the general manager of the orchestra, says the acoustics meant the musicians were unable to hear each other on stage. The sound in the hall travelled to the roof, making it difficult to balance and project the music.

JUNE 30   Wednesday: Media Release from Dr Andrew Refshauge, Deputy Premier and Minister for Urban Affairs and Planning, attributes the delay listing Opera House to Federal legislation:

The Premier, Mr Bob Carr, writes to the Prime Minister raising concerns about the implications of the Federal Government's *Environment Protection and Biodiversity Conservation Bill*. This Bill, currently before the House of Representatives, cedes power to the Commonwealth over sites listed on the world heritage register. The state government has received Crown Law advice that it is possible the new Federal legislation may grant control of the Opera House and its setting to the Commonwealth. The Premier writes to Mr Howard asking that negotiations begin on a bilateral agreement to guarantee major decisions about the Opera House remain the prerogative of the people of NSW and their representatives.

Media Release concludes: *'Once the terms of the bilateral agreement have been finalised the NSW government will ask the Commonwealth to formally nominate the Opera House and its setting for world heritage listing.'*

JULY 1   NSW Heritage Office, Parramatta, holds discussions between the commonwealth and NSW governments to finalise management and financial arrangements for the property in order to forward a nomination to UNESCO by 1 July 1999.

AUG 8   Sunday: Jan Utzon faxes message from Jørn Utzon regarding his appointment as design consultant to work on the Statement of Design Principles for the Sydney Opera House. Utzon says he hopes future architects would not be locked into the past in their approach to the building and instead make use of technology to find solutions: *'I like to think the Sydney Opera House is like a musical instrument and like any fine instrument it needs a little maintenance and fine tuning, from time to time, if it is to keep on performing at the highest level'*. Utzon also makes it clear he would not be seeking to redesign the present interior: *'My job is to articulate overall vision and detailed design principles for the site and for the form of the building and its interior.'* The Opera House chairman, Joseph Skrzynski, says later the interior will not be rebuilt to the original plan.

AUG 11   Wednesday: **Joseph Skrzynski**, speaking at the announcement of a formal agreement between Jørn Utzon and the SOH Trust, on the terms of the design brief, states his appointment as a design consultant to the Sydney Opera House, is for a sum understood to be about $300,000 (but rumoured to much higher). *'This appointment is a historically necessary reconciliation and will ensure that any future changes to the Sydney Opera House or its site will be consistent with Utzon's design principles.'* He says Utzon will work on the brief in association with Richard Johnson of the firm DCM. *'The Statement of Design Principles will fully document the design concept and details for the Sydney Opera House, and will be published as a permanent reference for the long–term conservation and management of the building.'* He added it will serve as a prime reference document for any proposal for change affecting the building and its site. This would take six months and be ready by February 2000. In the document describing *The Strategic Planning Process*, it is stated that Utzon will not return to Sydney and that his son and partner, Jan Utzon, will prepare the *Statement of Design Principles*.

AUG 17   Tuesday, 12.30 p.m.: Launch of Philip Drew, *The Masterpiece*, biography of Utzon by Frank Sartor, Sydney Lord Mayor, introduced by Jennifer Byrne, host of ABC's Foreign Correspondent programme, in the SOH's Bennelong Restaurant.

SEPT 28   Richard Johnson suggests the replacement of the glass walls with the 'light hanging curtains of glass' which he says Utzon intended.

NOV 9   Tuesday: Lecture on the Sydney Opera House by Richard Johnson of DCM architects for the upgrade no. 2 at State Library of NSW. Johnson announces *'We expect (Utzon's) statement to be finished in the first half of next year'*, adding, *'It will become the permanent reference of all conservation.'* He confirms that the retired 81–year old architect will not travel to Australia because of concerns for his health. It is revealed that the SOH will cost up to $200 million to maintain over the next 10 to 20 years. The total expense of the new masterplan has yet to be determined.

NOV 29   Monday: Talk at Royal Australian Instiute of Architests, Tusculum, by Richard Johnson (DCM) reveals that Utzon is 'warming to the idea of more active involvement.' and indicates *'He will consider taking an area of the building and either reconstructing his original interior or a new one.'* Utzon is hopeful that his furniture designs for both the public and back–of–house spaces can be produced, since prototypes already exist.

'Utzon is not so much interested in going back to the original, as going back to the spirit of the original to produce something new,' Johnson says.

2000

JAN 1 The Opera House features in a 25–hour world wide television broadcast reaching more than 2 billion people. Satellite links bring concerts together at Sydney Opera House, Times Square, the Golden Gate Bridge, the Great Wall of China, the Taj Mahal, the Eiffel Tower, the Acropolis and the Great Pyramids by The Millennium Society to celebrate the first day of the 21st century. Inside the Concert Hall, Fanfare for the New Millennium entertains guests who pay up to $2000 with the stars of the Australian Opera, conducted by Simone Young and directed by Stuart Maunder. Also, 16,000 attend all–night party plus free party on the forecourt and Opera House steps.

FEB 15 SOH is proclaimed the only 20th century structure worthy of the title 'true millennium building' by Richard Weston, a professor at Cardiff University, UK, in an article in the RIBA Journal, 106/12, December 1999.

MAR 20 Her Majesty Queen Elizabeth II, accompanied by the Duke of Edinburgh, is greeted by 10,000 loyalists at SOH ceremony on a sodden wet Monday and meets Council for Aboriginal Reconciliation chair Evelyn Scott.

MAY 6 Utzon tells his son, Jan, that it is impractical to reinstate the original stage plans to accommodate regular opera productions in the main auditorium. He says that it is probably too late for his celebrated concept of 'glass walls' infilling the main openings at either ends of the vaults to be realised because this would involve closing the building for an unrealistic period. Jan Utzon insists Utzon will not return to Sydney because of he currently suffers from high blood pressure.

JUNE 27 **Tuesday: Completion of the human genome sequencing project of 3.1 billion subsets of the human gene by two teams, Dr Francis Collins heading the publicly funded Human Genome Project and Dr Craig Venter, managing director of Celera Genomics. The mapping of the human genome has been compared to putting a man on the moon said Dr Dexter, director of the Welcome Trust in UK.**

JUNE 28 Wednesday: 12.30–2.00 pm Reception for the 60 Council members of the International Union of Architects (UIA) on the occasion of their meeting in Sydney in the Northern Foyer Lounge of the Opera Theatre hosted by Andrew Refshauge, Minister for Urban Affairs & Planning. Howard still refuses to forward the World Heritage Nomination of SOH to Paris. Submission of Utzon guidelines further delayed to late 2000; no final date is given.

JULY 1 **Saturday: introduction of a 10% Goods & Services Tax (GST) by Howard government.**

JUL 28 Friday: Sir Leslie (John) Martin, one of four jourors for the Sydney Opera House competition dies at Cambridge (b. Manchester 17 Aug 1908) aged 91.

JULY 29 Saturday: Second production of *The Eighth Wonder* opens in Opera Theatre, SOH; Utzon is played by Grant Smith. Runs till 18 August with 5 performances.

| **AUG 18** | 2000 Olympic Arts Festival opens with Opera Australia production of *Don Giovanni* by Mozart. |

SEPT 15 **Friday: Opening Ceremony, Olympic Stadium, Homebush, of the XXVIIth Sydney 2000 Olympic Games.** At dusk, swimmer Samantha Riley stands on top of the north apex of the concert hall arc of the Opera House roof and holds the torch aloft on the final leg of the flame's journey to Stadium Australia for the opening ceremony.

SEPT 16 Triathlon starts and finishes at the Sydney Opera House Forecourt Women (Sep 16) Men (Sep 17).

OCT 1 **Sunday: Closing ceremony in the Olympic Stadium (day 16).**

APPENDIX A:

CHANGES TO SYDNEY OPERA HOUSE FROM 1973 TO 2000

THE CONCERT HALL

(seating capacity 2679, used for symphony, jazz and popular music concerts); stage area 17–11m x 11.5m deep. The room acoustics were assisted by 21 adjustable acrylic acoustic clouds suspended on stainless steel cables above the concert platform.

1986 – 87	6 hydraulic scissor lifts installed under the stage to assist multi–level platform requirements for orchestral and choral concerts.
1988 – 89	recoating of the birch veneer wall and ceiling panels.
1991 – 92	flexibility achieved by 5 hydraulic lifts which replace the earlier temporary extensions to the stage.
1994 – 95	stage clouds replaced by a similar but stronger set.
1996 – 97	internal moulded plywood wall and ceiling panels refurbished, ceiling supports strengthened.
1997 – 98	acoustic study carried out with input from major users, led to primary recommendation of a reflector over the stage.
1998 – 99	increasing public debate on the acoustic qualities of the Concert Hall results in funds being set aside for an acoustic study
	during 1999–2000, air–conditioning upgrade to reduce energy consumption.

OPERA THEATRE

(seating capacity 1567) used for opera and ballet. Total area of 437m^2, performance area 316m^2, proscenium 12m x 7m high. Sets moved vertically on large lifts to scene dock below).

1973	Orchestra pit initially accommodated maximum of 75 musicians. Its platforms can be raised to provide 28m^2 additional stage.
1978 – 79	Orchestra pit enlarged 'as much as possible'.
1988 & 1992	further changes to pit, opening enlarged by 0.5m along its length together with improvements to the pit balustrade.
1993 – 94	pit enlarged and sight lines improved by reduction and relocation of columns (1995 Nov – $840,000).
1994 – 95	Stage 2 of pit extension completed increasing area from 105m^2 to 143m^2 results in demolition of existing pit and building of new structure. Funds set aside for acoustics study.

DRAMA THEATRE

(seating capacity 550, used for plays)

MUSIC ROOM

(original seating capacity 420, used principally for chamber music, solo recitals, film screenings and small conventions)

1979   Becomes a cinema, used primarily for film screenings, also continues as a theatre

1984   Becomes a playhouse used primarily as a theatre, seating capacity reduced to 398 with stage 12m wide x 5m deep, proscenium 5.5m high.

REHEARSAL AND RECORDING HALL

(located immediately below Concert Hall stage and originally intended for the Major Hall stage machinery. Area 641m² with 3 galleries on three sides. Equipped with facilities for direct radio and television broadcasts and making recordings. Used initially for performances and rehearsals by orchestras and choirs).

1986   Becomes Broadwalk Studio, new mobile retractable seating for 288 people installed.

1989   Becomes Dennis Wolanski Library of the Performing Arts, originally as a temporary measure to facilitate construction below Exhibition Hall/Library space and provide accommodation for Public Works Department. In addition, the Broadwalk Studio did not comply with new fire regulations and required heavy subsidization in a time of acute budgetary pressures.

1992–95   TheatreWorks proposal emerged as a solution to provide the House with a permanent daytime attraction and source of revenue.

1999   Becomes the Studio to 'encourage the development of emerging artists and art forms and provide an opportunity to forge stronger links with the industry'.

EXHIBITION HALL

(area 650m²)

1973   Intended for exhibitions of painting, sculpture, photographs, artifacts, theatre memorabilia, trade shows.

1975 Dec Divided into two areas to accommodate the Dennis Wolansky Library & Archives of the Performing Arts.

1978   Utzon museum: Jørn Utzon urges the establishment of a *'small museum in Sydney to house the plans for the building. I would like people to be able to see my plans…'*

1988–89   Building of the Century exhibition (attendance 78,000).

1989   Leif Kristensen submits proposals and drawings for a museum and cafe in the gardens, adjacent to the Man O'War steps to house a permanent exhibition on the history, design and construction of the House.

1989–93   Playhouse backstage facilities, catering and construction areas.

1994–95   *Unseen Utzon* exhibition (attendance 25,500). Utzon donates 1965 model of the Major Hall interior to the Trust.

1995–   used as office accommodation for Theatre Department.

FOYERS

1995 –   Cafe Mozart created and enlarged into cloakroom, Box Office Foyer Shop.

1997 Dec – 99 Western Broadwalk Foyer (L. Kristensen architect) opened.

RESTAURANTS

Bennelong Restaurant – early proposal for music library

1988 Jan   Concourse Restaurant opened.

1995 Aug   Bennelong Restaurant refurbished to seat 100 ($1.3M)

1998 – 99   Green Room servery and bar upgraded, new carpet

EXTERIOR

1995 Feb $6.5 million spent over 18 months on resealing 16.5km of joints between tile lids.

SYDNEY OPERA HOUSE CAR PARK

1960 March   Utzon proposal for car park capacity 1,100 vehicles under Royal Botanical Gardens.

1964 June   Blue Book proposal is rejected.

1973 – 85   Forecourt and part of the RB Gardens used as car park, use of Gardens is extended to 1993.

1993 March   Underground carpark in Royal Botanic Gardens, 1,100 car park built and operated by Enacon Parking Pty Ltd is completed at cost of $40M under a 50 year lease arrangement. On 11 levels, spiral access ramp to a depth of 33m.

FORECOURT/LOWER CONCOURSE DEVELOPMENT/RETAIL

1993   asphalt paved with metal covered walkway

1988   Second glass and steel covered walkway (1988–$34.6M) built to connect Circular Quay Station with new multilevel forecourt development which included a lower concourse arcade with restaurant, shops, offices and toilets.

1988   AC Lewis Fountain installed at roadway entrance, Macquarie St.

1997 – 98 Nov $650M re–development of East Circular Quay for 237 apartments, 700 seat arthouse cinema, fashion stores and 9 eateries.

1988   glass covered walkway is demolished and replaced by colonnade connection under the new development.

APPENDIX B:

SYDNEY OPERA HOUSE ESTIMATES AND REAL COSTS

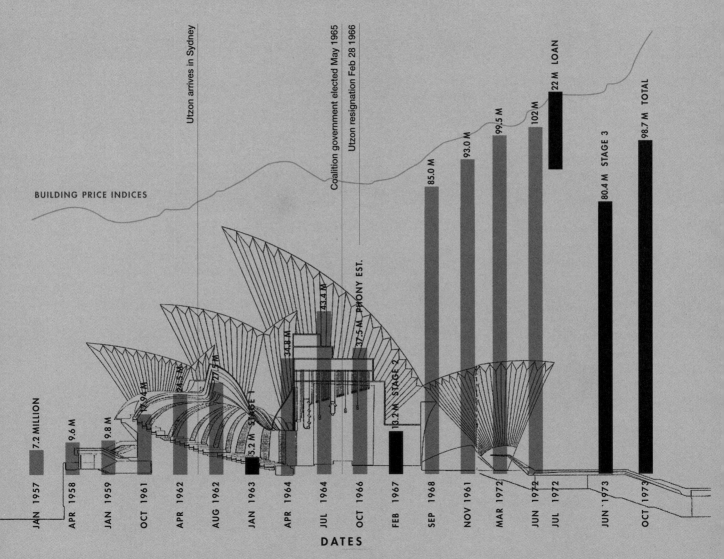

Utzon arrives in Sydney

Coalition government elected May 1965

Utzon resignation Feb 28 1966

BUILDING PRICE INDICES

22 M LOAN

102 M

99.5 M

93.0 M

85.0 M

98.7 TOTAL

80.4 M STAGE 3

43.4 M

37.5 M PHONY EST.

34.8 M

27.5 M

29.5 M

23.94 M

13.2 M STAGE 2

9.8 M

9.6 M

7.2 MILLION

5.2 M STAGE 1

| JAN 1957 | APR 1958 | JAN 1959 | OCT 1961 | APR 1962 | AUG 1962 | JAN 1963 | APR 1964 | JUL 1964 | OCT 1966 | FEB 1967 | SEP 1968 | NOV 1961 | MAR 1972 | JUN 1972 | JUL 1972 | JUN 1973 | OCT 1973 |

DATES

INDEX

Page numbers in *italics* refer to illustrations

143, 144, 145, 147, 148, 149, 151, 154; 2000 Olympic Games 159; State Office Building 119

Sydney Opera House:

acoustics 59, 79, 95, 97, 100, 104, 105, 122, 143; Broadwalk Studio 137, 146, 154, 155; Bennelong Restaurant *57*, 141; Brown book 41; changes to 121, APPENDIX A, 160–2; Committee (SOHEC) 39, 42, 48, 49, 76; competition 12, 40, 41, capsule 42; Cost blow–out 125, 126, 128; Cost Estimates 6, 52, 82, 84, 91, 92, 93, 95, 102, 123, APPENDIX B, 163; early proposals 25, 32, 33, 39; Final cost 130, 133; first performances capsule 131; Forecourt 135, 136; formwork 80; glass walls 91, 95, 99, 100; Gold book 56; library 143; lottery & funding 47, 49, 54, 93, 130, 136; Major Hall design 82, 86, 88, 90, 92, 122; Millennium celebration 158; Minor Hall design 91, 92, *101*; 'October Scheme' 54; opening 130; Opera House Trust Act 63, 64, 73, 83; National Opera House competition 41, *43, 44;* organ 133; parking 61, 93, 99, 100, 104, 139; Parliamentary Acts 119, 120, 124; plywood 64, 82, 86, 88, 91, 96, 98, 99, 104, 106; pop concert 103; rebuilding 144; Red book 52, 56; restaurant *57*; roof schemes *63, 65, 68, 69, 70*, 74, 76; site selection 39, 40; spherical geometry 82, 85; staged construction 52, 96; stage machinery 96, 100; structural check 82; tiles 79, 104, 146; Utzon Museum 137; *The Eighth Wonder* opera 142, 158; Sydney Opera House Trust (SOHT) 73–4; Upgrade 1 138, 140, 142, 145; Upgrade 2 144, 146, capsule 147, 148, 149, 151, 153; World Heritage Listing 141, 143, 147–8, 152, 156, 158; Yellow book 79; Sydney Opera House Executive Committee (SOHEC) 81, 85, 95

Sydney Opera House Society 6, 124

Symonds, Ralph 53, 60, 72, 80, 88, 90, 95, 98, 99, 100

T

Takeyama, Minoru 82

Thomas, James 61, 71

Thompson, R.M. 83, 91

Todd, Lionel 143, 148

U

Unruh, Dr. Walter 59, 61, 67, 72, 82

Utsep Mobler Flexible Furniture 123

Utzon, Aage Oberg 23, 126

Utzon, ancestors, capsule 19, surname 18

Utzon, Erik Oberg 24, 33, 38, 40

Utzon, Estrid Halina 23, 36

Utzon Foundation 151, 153

Utzon–Frank, Einar 23

Utzon, Jan Oberg 30, 135, 156, 158

Utzon, Kim Oberg 42, 84, 105

Utzon, Leif Oberg 29, 91

Utzon, Lin Oberg 32, 84, 98, 103, 125, 134, 135, 136, 138, 139, 141, 146, 153

Utzon, Jørn

Oberg, Aalto Medal 135; ancestors capsule 19; criticism 7; departure 8; fees 8, 102, 103, 104, 112, 115, 125; furniture, 33, 63, 97, 123, 125; houses 93, 96, 97, 102; land deals 73, 74, 82, 84, 90, 97, 119, 128; 9–points demands 108, 111; offices 74, 83, 84, 95, (Sydney) capsule 108; patents 55, 63, 86, 90; plagiarism 33; rejoins SOH 154, 157; Sonning Prize 149, *150*; statement to Davis Hughes capsule 113; tax problems 8, 107, 122, 123; training 25, 30; withdrawal *9*, 107, 112, 114; yachts 90, 126

V

Vienna, Burgtheater 51, 67, 81; Staatsoper 51, 66–7

Vietnam War 82, 93, 98, 99, 125, 126, 128, 141

W

Waagner–Biro 53, 60, 64, 66, 71, 72, 96

Weatherburn, Charles 110, 115, 118

Weston, Prof Richard 158

Wheatland, W.W. 85, 96, 107, 114, 115, 116, 121

White, Patrick 83, 84

Whitlam, Edward Gough 128

Wolf Foundation Prize 138, 139

Wolfsburg, Theatre 117

Wood, William Walter capsule 91, 100, 106

Wran, Neville 135

Wright, Frank Lloyd 17, 35, 36, 49

Y

Yamasaki, Minoru 49

Yucatan 35, 117

Z

Zeuthen & Søensen 80

Zunz, Sir Jack capsule 74, 76, 79–80, 81, 83, 85, 106, 117

Zürich, Schauspielhaus competition 86, 90, 91, 92, *94*, 95, 99, 124, 125, 128, 133